Praise for . . .
Me, Inc.

♛

"Scott Ventrella takes best practices of Fortune 500 companies and shows how you can apply them to another important venture — you! Your life deserves at least as much attention as your job does, so read this book and turn your time on earth into a satisfying, meaningful enterprise."

> Ken Blanchard, co-author of
> *The One Minute Manager*® and
> *Leading at a Higher Level*

"Rarely does a book so authentically capture the essence of what true 'personal brand' transformation is all about. *Me, Inc.* provides a unique approach to discovering your personal brand and making it a reality. Through Scott's insights and invaluable self-discovery tools, readers quickly learn that when you build your personal brand, you build a brand of value . . . value that eloquently translates into success throughout every facet of your life."

> Laura Tessinari, Senior Partner,
> Director of Training, Ogilvy & Mather

"The Me, Inc. program has guided me on the path to even greater personal and professional achievement and life satisfaction than I ever thought possible."

> Jack Hallahan, Vice President,
> Advertising and Brand Partnerships, MobiTV

"In all of the 13 years since I first heard Scott speak on this subject, I have consistently been impressed by the value of his approach and the responses of the hundreds of students who have benefited from his structured program. With the publication of *Me, Inc.*, Scott now reveals to a much larger audience the ways of creating successful, happy lives [that] his students at Fordham and his executive coaching clients have been applying with excellent results for years."

Professor James A.F. Stoner,
Fordham University Graduate School of Business,
New York City

"*Me, Inc.* provides a clear road map to achieving your goals and finding greater work-life balance. Ventrella's approach offers an interesting and powerful way to assume control; by managing your life's ambitions as seriously as you might a business endeavor, you can clarify your thoughts, set priorities and turn your dreams into reality. Ventrella is a very effective coach and, like any good boss, he doesn't let you off the hook. You want to change things? Look no further."

Teri Schindler, Media Consultant,
Patrick Davis Partners

ME, INC.

How to Master the Business of Being You

A Personalized Program for Exceptional Living

SCOTT W. VENTRELLA

JOHN WILEY & SONS, INC.

*To my wife and best friend, Catherine
And our two precious children,
Jennifer and Andrew*

You and I possess within ourselves,
at every moment of our lives, under all circumstances,
the power to transform the quality of our lives.

—*Werner Erhard*

Contents

Phase III:
Turning Your Plan into Reality

Phase IV:
Keeping Your Momentum Going

Introduction

Living on Purpose

Yes, You Can Have the Exceptional Life You've Always Dreamed Of

If you were the CEO of a mediocre company, what would you do? Would you idly watch money drain away like water through a sieve? Would you silently stand by while your employees walked out the door or your stock hovered uncomfortably below market? Of course you wouldn't. You'd make a plan to reinvigorate the business. And you'd implement the plan. In other words, you'd *actively manage* the business.

Well, you know what? Whether you like it or not, you *are* the CEO of Me, Inc. You've already been hired to master the business of being you. The key question is: what kind of leadership role have you taken in your own life? Do you feel satisfied by your work? Are you happy with your family? Are you finding a balance between your own needs and the needs of others? Are you accomplishing your goals? Are you leading the life you want to be leading—an exceptional life, and not just an average one?

Since you're in charge, why not strive to be just as efficient, effective, successful, attentive, and thorough in running your life as you can be? Why *not* treat your whole life like it's the most important job you've ever had?

You may be thinking up all kinds of excuses right now, like "I'm just too busy" or "I've got more important things to do than think about my dreams and why I seem to have forgotten to pursue them somewhere along the way." But what could possibly be *more* worth your time and effort than leading an exceptional life? It's time for you to start taking Me, Inc. seriously. Like a top-performing business, you need to stop doing things by accident and start *living on purpose.* You alone are ultimately responsible for your own life. So why not embrace your role with enthusiasm and determination, confident that you can do the job — and do it well.

Think of *Me, Inc.* as a workbook for helping you manage the business of living. With the guidance and hands-on activities provided in *Me, Inc.*, you can move from an average to an exceptional life in just 16 weeks. But unlike many self-help books, which are really polemics about the *need* for purpose or goals, this book is action-oriented. You won't just sit down and read it; you'll actually *do* it. In every chapter, you'll find activities for you to complete as you go.

What's more, the tools are based on principles that have been proven effective time and again in the business world, as well as in the lives of people I know. In short, *Me, Inc.* works. The business techniques presented here consistently improve product quality, customer service, and bottom-line performance at Fortune 500 companies, and they prove to be equally effective in your personal life. I've watched as hundreds of my students and clients have successfully employed this methodology to create and implement **Exceptional Living Plans** — specific, individualized strategies that have changed their lives for the better.

Finally, this book doesn't offer some generic plan that you're supposed to follow just because I tell you to. This is no salesman's snake oil, no witch doctor's magical cure-all elixir. On the contrary, *Me, Inc.* provides you with the tools that enable you to develop a plan that *you* write, that's based on *your* values and priorities, and works within the framework *you* determine, according to *your* timeline, to get *you living the life you want.* So by the end, you'll have an Exceptional Living Plan *in action.*

I have a message for you: You *can* have the exceptional life you've always dreamed of living. All you need to do is manage your life as if it were your business. It *is* your business, after all, isn't it? So sit up straight, take a deep breath, and get ready to take charge of Me, Inc.

Real Life, Real Results

Susan had the glamorous job in publishing, the cozy family, and the enviable Central Park West apartment, but none of it felt as good as it sounded. Although she had set out after college to have a meaningful, satisfying, and even extraordinary life, she found herself at age 42 feeling as if her life were merely passable. After 17 years her work as

a powerful publishing executive did not inspire or challenge her anymore, her daughter was about to leave the
nest for college, and she and her husband had been focused on child rearing for so long that they were more co-
parents than a couple. What's more, lately she had been
cringing at the sound of car horns and lamenting the
lack of trees in New York City. Had she lost her way somewhere? Had she unnecessarily accepted the life she had?
Could she do better if she only knew how?

As a life strategy and executive coach, I work with
people like Susan, helping them to gain transformative insights into themselves, reinvigorate their lives, and learn
how to live life intentionally rather than passively. When
she first walked into my office, Susan said, "Help! I don't
know what I want to be and do next. It's not just that I don't
know how to get there. It's that I don't even know where
there is. All I know is that I want it to be better than *here*."

My response took Susan off guard. "It's time to start
treating your life like it's your business," I told her. And
then I explained. Here's what I've discovered in my 25
years of work as a therapist and life strategy coach to individual clients wanting more from their lives, a consultant
to complacent multibillion-dollar corporations, and a lec-
turer to overwhelmed students at Harvard, Dartmouth,
Columbia, and Fordham universities: *You can use the best
techniques from business to obtain clarity, create change,
achieve fulfillment, grow relationships, and reach goals in
your personal life.*

The healthiest, most successful companies — like the

ones listed in *Fortune* magazine's "Best Companies to Work For" survey every year — are the envy of everyone who doesn't work for them because they insist on being exceptional instead of merely good enough. They offer flexibility; foster a fun, creative workplace environment; are ethical, family oriented, socially responsible; know what they're about; and treat their people well. These companies assume that happy, focused, inspired employees work harder and better, and they're right: They get extraordinary results.

Why can't you have a life like that? A life that inspires you to be your best? I'm not proposing that you make your life more like a business, but rather that you can use some of the best ideas from the most successful companies (such as identifying a vision, setting and achieving goals that reflect that vision, taking great care of customers, actively managing crisis when it inevitably arises, and communicating with and empowering others) to get better organized, live more authentically, navigate transitions, and achieve greater balance in your life. And I've developed a program that will help you do exactly that.

Once I'd explained the background and basics of the Me, Inc. program to Susan, we were ready to begin. I quickly discovered that she is accustomed to defining herself as a successful professional. And with good reason: She's smart, talented, and used to getting what she wants. So at first she kept obsessing over her "final destination" — determining what her new career should be. She talked about reinventing herself.

"Slow down," I told her. "Let's not forget about your family and your living arrangements in this process. I'm not a career counselor; I'm a life strategy coach. I want you to consider the big picture, your *total quality way of life*. First, we're going to focus on your identity. Once you figure out *who* you are, then you can figure out what you want to do and how you're going to get there. We have to deconstruct you before we can reconstruct you."

Susan looked surprised—again. So I went on, "You can't successfully reinvent your life, you can't make it *feel* the way you want it to, until you have a sense of your core values. A business wouldn't start up without defining its mission, would it? So let's start by talking about what matters most to you: Contributing financially? Supporting your husband and daughter in their lives? Winning awards in your career? Being able to say yes to any friend or family member who needs your help? Fighting for a cause? When you look at yourself in terms of who you want to be, you may find yourself opening up to dozens of options that you previously never would have considered."

I had Susan start by writing what I call a Platinum Standard, a statement that describes the essence of who we are and our overarching values. Hers was "To lead a high-impact, rewarding and fulfilling life and to be an outstanding mother and wife and to contribute to society by empowering others." From this, she determined her top priorities, which included finding and beginning a stimulating new career while being available to her family and taking care of her own health.

Next, we evaluated why she's dissatisfied with her current job. It had left her feeling stifled and constrained, like she was the only one in the office who wanted to take risks. She wanted more freedom, the opportunity to explore her creativity. Based on this information, we were able to come up with ideas for what kind of career she'd be happy pursuing, and concluded that she would be most satisfied working as a freelance writer. She enjoys challenging work, but is willing to compromise on salary and seniority; money and a prestigious title aren't as important to her now as they were when she was in her 20s and 30s. Plus, if she works fewer hours than she did in the past, she'll have more time to focus on her other priorities, including maintaining strong relationships with her daughter and husband. We also talked about how she needs to find time for herself in this new life.

Next, we mapped out in detail how Susan will move forward from here. We did this not in the abstract sense, but by creating an actual business plan for Susan's life. Her Exceptional Living Plan has categories for relationships, career, personal satisfaction, and health, ordered according to her priorities. She has set goals in each category and established reasonable timelines for what she will achieve by when. I asked her to keep on top of her goals, always updating her plan and reporting back to me honestly on her progress, just as an employee would report back honestly to her boss.

Since creating her plan, Susan has quit her job and tells me that she's been able to develop her freelance writing into a full-time but not overly consuming career, one in which she is able to determine her workload on a month-to-month basis. She and her husband have sold their apartment in New York City and moved to a small but comfortable house upstate near a placid lake. Susan enjoys having more free time to exercise, relax, and explore life in her new town. She's still figuring things out with her husband and misses her daughter terribly, but just having a plan in hand makes her feel a million times better. It gives her a sense of control. She's leading her life; it's not leading her. And even better, she's living the life she imagined.

Living Your Life in the Purpose Zone

Why do you need *Me, Inc.*? Because chances are, you're not leading the best possible life you could be living. And *no one* sets out to live a mediocre life. It just happens to us along the way. But it doesn't have to remain so. I think people are always living in one of three zones: the **Complacency Zone,** the **Crisis Zone,** or the **Purpose Zone.**

Like Susan, people living in the Complacency Zone are stuck in the status quo — even though they're not happy about it. When you're in the Complacency Zone, it's as though you're aimlessly drifting along a river, letting the currents take you where they may. You could make an effort to set and reach goals, but you aren't motivated to do so. Or you're always making excuses for yourself: You're too busy, or it's never the right time. I have a TV producer friend, Sarah, who is living in the Complacency Zone. She wants to be in front of the camera, not behind it. But instead of going for it, she's always telling me, "Not now. I'm putting together this piece that's due soon," or "As soon as the November sweeps are over," or "Next month I'll talk to my boss about it." So it still hasn't happened.

The Complacency Zone is a dangerous place to be. Like the Free Parking space in Monopoly, it feels safe, but hanging out there for too long means that you're missing the game. After all, you may not be drifting in the right direction. Perhaps you've become intoxicated by superficial signs of success — you've got a nice house, the right car, fine clothes — but underneath, you're disaffected and dissatisfied with your life. Or perhaps you're ignoring the needs of those people who are most important to you. If you're in the Complacency Zone, you risk finding yourself at age 70 asking, "What have I done with my life?" Or worse, waking up one day to find that your husband is threatening to leave you, or your kid has a drug problem, or you're being fired for sloppy work. Suddenly you're in the Crisis Zone.

People in the Crisis Zone are hemorrhaging but often don't know what to fix first. Maybe they've spent too much time in the Complacency Zone, not paying attention. Or maybe they've just hit a particularly rough patch in the road. If you're in the Crisis Zone, you frequently feel lost and overwhelmed. You don't have enough time or energy to plan for the future because you're too busy just trying to make it through the current crisis so that you can tackle the next. Exercise more often? You can barely find the time to eat lunch.

The Crisis Zone is an extremely stressful place to be. People who linger here often end up self-destructing—jobs, relationships, and other projects go up in flames. If you're in the Crisis Zone, you need to take action fast.

You want to be living in the Purpose Zone. If you're in the Purpose Zone, as many of the people I have coached over the years are now that they've completed the Me, Inc. program, you've already mapped out your course. You're actively guiding your life toward your desired destination. If problems arise, you know how to fix them. Having an Exceptional Living Plan is like having a compass when you're lost: It's always pointing due north, even if you're not, so you can simply take a read and get back on course.

Steve offers an excellent example of someone who moved from the Crisis and Complacency Zones and into the Purpose Zone by applying the process described in *Me, Inc.* to his life. At age 37, Steve had been living in the Complacency Zone for years. A workaholic engineer, he'd been drifting along without really thinking about where he was going. Then one day, life got worse. His wife left him after years of disconnection and, as a result, he became distanced from his three-year-old son. Steve also realized that he was working long hours at a job he disliked. "My life was a mess," he said. "I didn't even know where to start."

Steve was in the Crisis Zone.

That's when he enrolled in the course I teach based

on this material at New York City's Fordham University. He wrote a mission statement — a Platinum Standard — set short- and long-term goals, and created a concrete Exceptional Living Plan for making his vision a reality.

A year later, Steve has met and even exceeded most of his goals. He loves his new job, which is less demanding of his time. He's taking better care of himself — meditating for fifteen minutes before going to bed at night, and eating breakfast in the morning. He's spending weekends with his son, and their relationship has grown as a result. What's more, Steve is dating a wonderful woman, Julie, which he also attributes to Me, Inc. "If I hadn't taken the course, I wouldn't have made the time to meet new people. Plus I wouldn't have been as open and honest with Julie about what I want out of life. It's one of the things that initially attracted her to me," he explains.

Steve admits that he is still struggling with his workaholic tendencies. But overall, he feels that he is on a clear path to his exceptional life. "Just making a commitment to a simple statement like 'I want to be happy with where I am' was monumental. It made me conscious of factors that need to be included in all my decisions."

Steve is a new man — a man living in the Purpose Zone.

Which zone are you in right now? And where would you like to be? Most of us don't exist in one zone all the time. But I'm certain that if you spend a few moments thinking about it, you can identify the zone you're in the *majority* of the time. If you're not in the Purpose Zone, or if you've too often found yourself slipping into the Complacency or Crisis Zones, this book is for you. If you find that you do spend most of your time in the Purpose Zone but that there are one or two areas of your life where you feel you have room for improvement, then *Me, Inc.* can help you, too.

Planning for Success

The meaning of "success" is changing — for the better. Due to a number of social, economic, and technological factors, people today are redefining what success looks like for them as individuals in their private and professional lives. And on the whole, the emphasis is shifting from *quantity* to *quality*. Put another way, in this day and age success is becoming less about how *much* we have in life and more about how *well* we're living our lives.

For most of the previous century, success was determined primarily by the accumulation of things — money, credentials, status symbols, and power. The problem is that people who bought into the quantity success formula are now finding that once they've achieved their goals, life often seems empty and unfulfilled. They experience a lack of joy, happiness, and peace. That's because the attainment of things generally came at the expense of crucial quality factors. Decades of need and greed have contributed to the deterioration of our relationships, health, and self-esteem. Divorce rates have increased exponentially. Health and well-being, both physical and mental, have declined in spite of medical advances. The prescription drug business is booming; there's a pill for every imaginable ache and pain. Unprecedented numbers of people of all ages are seeking or receiving therapy.

Fortunately, we are waking up from our slumber. Growing numbers of people are realizing that they've been missing out on the important things in life. Recently, I was talking to a businessman who said that although he likes his job, it has been all consuming, sapping him of his energy and spirit. He works very long hours, travels extensively, and finds it difficult to relax even when not on the job. He told me, "I've been increasingly unhappy for the past several months and realized that I have not been able to enjoy life. So I've decided to make a conscious effort to spend more time with my wife and kids and take more time for myself." To be clear, he was not suggesting that he was going to quit his job. Instead, he was going to make a concerted effort to refocus some of his time and attention to meet his new priorities. That's an excellent start. But he — and you — can do better. We are all capable of making significant and lasting changes in our lives. A friend of mine, Olga, has developed her own personal definition of success: "Success is when you are happy to go to work in the morning and happy to come back in the evening, and you are very welcome and liked in both places." We are all capable of rediscovering and implementing our own personal meaning of success.

Are you, like Susan, feeling lost and confused because you don't know where your life is going? Did you, like

Steve, wake up one day to find your life falling to pieces because you weren't paying it enough attention? Perhaps you're about to get married or have kids, and you're trying to figure out how to make more time in your life for your loved ones. Or maybe you're facing divorce, illness, or loss, and you're looking for a way to cope with these changes. Maybe you're newly retired or your kids have just left home and you're wondering what's next. Perhaps you're seeking a new job or a new relationship, and you want to be more organized in how you go about it this time around. Do you have the sense that you aren't in control of what's happening anymore? Are you frustrated that you aren't living life to your full potential? Or do you know what you want to achieve, but aren't sure how to make it happen? *Me, Inc.* will help you create a plan to get back on track.

I'm not implying that your life is *totally* out of control. Like most of my clients and students and the businessman I just mentioned above, you're probably a successful person who just has a lot on your plate. You sometimes feel stressed out by the lack of balance in your life. But you're too smart to live chaotically by scraping through one emergency and then the next. And so you're looking for a bit of extra help so you can live the best life possible.

Even my younger friends, students, and acquaintances in the early stages of their careers are reevaluating their priorities and seeking greater personal fulfillment in life. Take Mia, a 29-year-old student of mine. Working part time, going to graduate school, and taking care of her aging parents has left her feeling completely overloaded. When asked to talk about the life she wants, she says, "More calm. And I'd like to have a job that pays more so I can afford some extra assistance with caring for my mom and dad." So I'm helping her put together a plan to do just that. Another one of my students, Alexander, just left a highly demanding job with a software developer. He felt that the long, hard hours he had put in over the past two years were already driving him to the point of burnout. He took my course at Fordham because he wanted to thoughtfully consider which next career choice would offer him greater balance in life.

A few months ago while speaking at a leadership conference at the Harvard Business School, I was asked by one of the students, "When should we start thinking about living according to the quality success principles you've just outlined?" I responded, "Yesterday, because it's never too soon." The longer we wait to build quality into the fabric of our lives, the more ingrained our current poor living habits become. Don't think that you can focus on the quantity now and get to the quality later — you may never have the chance.

It's inevitable that you're going to face tumultuous times of transition. After all, the only constant in life is change. You can't lead your life to such an extent that you're able to control everything that happens to you — no one can, not even the most wealthy, powerful person on the planet. Even Jennifer Aniston gets dumped. Even Prince William of England gets pimples. Even Oprah has bad days. But by doing the activities provided in *Me, Inc.*, you can discover how easy it is to be organized and effective about managing change. What's more, just by creating an Exceptional Living Plan, you'll help relieve a lot of your stress right away.

After completing the program, Susan told me, "Me, Inc. appeals to me because I'm the type of person who likes a plan. Some people prefer to live life in a very serendipitous way, but you know, even they need a plan sometimes, especially when they're off course. The thing is, having an Exceptional Living Plan doesn't mean your life can't be fun. It just means your life has more structure." I couldn't have put it better myself.

What's So Great about Business?

When I say that we can apply principles utilized by successful companies to our personal lives, I'm not suggesting that we should copy every wild idea or temporary trend that's ever been cooked up by corporate America. I'm suggesting that we can learn from business *best practices* — the benchmark concepts that people write books about and build respected, long-lasting, constantly evolving companies based upon. These principles, when applied on an individual level, can help make you the most effective "CEO" of your life that you can be. And when you've got things under control, when you're leading a life in the Purpose Zone, you'll find that you're able to reach new heights of career achievement and personal fulfillment.

Here are just a few examples of how healthy businesses solve problems and how individuals can utilize those same strategies:

- Excellent companies and exceptional individuals *have a vision*.
    - Companies create vision statements to guide them. If they don't, they find themselves drifting aimlessly like a ship without a rudder. Starbucks, for example, makes "contributing positively to our communities and our environment" the centerpiece of its vision. It ensures that all its products are created in environmentally sustainable ways, and it contributes to not-for-profit organizations that address social issues in its coffee origin countries.
    - Individuals also benefit from having a sense of purpose in life. We must make plans and set goals in order to reach our destination or we, too, will wander off course. We must be committed to what we believe in. Think of someone you admire: What is his or her guiding purpose? I bet you can see it manifest in the choices he or she makes on a daily basis. Just look at Steve. Once he defined his Platinum Standard as "Being happy with where I am right now," he started taking better care of his own health, working less, meeting new people, and growing closer to his son.
- Excellent companies and exceptional individuals *focus on their customers*.

- Companies like Stew Leonard's, an incredibly successful grocery store chain headquartered in Connecticut, stick by the slogan "The customer is always right." That's because they know that if they don't take the time to understand customer's needs and consistently deliver on those needs, they run the risk of losing that business — forever. Just think of how upset you get when a company doesn't answer its phones or a clerk treats you poorly. Stew Leonard's, on the other hand, wins remarkably high levels of employee and customer loyalty (and, as a result, profits) by treating people with the utmost respect.
- Similarly, we have important "customers" in our lives. If we don't take care of our loved ones, like Steve, we run the risk of losing these relationships — forever. We need to make sure that our most prized customers remain our top priority.

- Excellent companies and exceptional individuals *manage by fact.*
  - Companies rely on data that they've gathered and analyzed — not just instinct and spur-of-the-moment ideas — to make decisions. Jack Welch turned GE into a leading global company by demanding that his employees manage not by how they felt, but by what they actually saw happening.
  - In our personal lives, we often make tough decisions based on our "gut feel." And while these emotional reactions are important to consider, they do not necessarily guide us down the optimal path. We can

learn to solve problems by letting the facts of the situation light a clear path for us. My client Brian and his wife Joanna have learned to use this approach with many problems they confront in their personal lives. A few years ago, for example, Brian was traveling frequently for his consulting job and it was putting a strain on their marriage. They needed to find a way to spend more time together, but they both wanted Brian to be successful at his job, too. And so they dug into the bag of tricks offered in this book for a solution. They did what good businesses do when confronting a problem: They ran the numbers. For a month, they charted the number of nights Brian spent away from home. Then, together they created a target number for the following month. When Brian started approaching the maximum number of nights away, he began turning down consulting projects and coming home to Joanna instead. This concrete action plan worked wonders for the couple. Brian was able to manage his workload better, and Joanna appreciated having a say in how much time he spent on the road. Brian and Joanna practiced good business, and in so doing they were able to find their way to a solution.

- Excellent companies and exceptional individuals *empower people*.
  - Companies enable all employees to make decisions in order to bring out the best in people and ensure an optimal allocation of resources. The Ritz-Carlton

hotel chain is famous for this. Every staff member, from desk clerk to maid, has the authority to deliver on guests' requests — without first needing to gain approval from a manager. This policy makes both guests and employees happy: The guests get what they want, fast, and the employees feel that their company trusts them and values their opinions.

- We often try to do everything for everyone, and then complain that we don't have enough time for our families or for ourselves. By empowering others to take on certain responsibilities, such as helping out with housework or financial planning, we free ourselves to devote time and attention to what matters most. We also develop the skills and build the self-esteem of those whom we empower.

- Excellent companies and exceptional individuals *never stop trying to improve*.

  - Companies know that if they become complacent, their competition will take over. And so they foster the attitude that "things can always be better." Motorola saved itself from the brink of bankruptcy in the mid-1980s by adopting this attitude. The Japanese electronics industry was beating the socks off of the company at the time. The consulting firm I was working for, Juran Institute, coached then-CEO Bob Galvin to turn things around. Together, we created a new vision for Motorola based on continuous improvement: Every product could be enhanced, and only perfection would do. As a result, Motorola started producing quality products on a par with those being manufactured by its Japanese competitors. It successfully regained market share, and maintains a solid business to this day.

- While it's important to appreciate contentment, it's also healthy to challenge ourselves to reach new heights. Rather than accepting things as they are, we can adopt an attitude that we can always improve ourselves, and therefore the lives of those around us. We can always reach further out of complacency and into the Purpose Zone, as Susan and Steve have been doing since they completed their Exceptional Living Plans.

In the final analysis, all business is deeply personal. In fact, organizational behavior is essentially about the way in which individuals conduct themselves as they collectively work toward common business goals. Throughout this book, I will be drawing on examples from companies to illustrate how a principle might be applied in the personal realm. Self-improvement, at the individual as well as the organizational level, is a highly introspective process. I encourage you to pause frequently as you read to reflect, listen to your heart and mind, and share with those you are closest to.

Where Do I Get This Stuff?

I've been progressively developing the materials presented in *Me, Inc.* over the past 25 years. The principles I explore and the real-life examples I provide to illustrate them are based on my extensive experience working with organizations as well as individuals as a business consultant, professor, and life coach.

After college, I completed a master's degree in psychology and started working as a therapist, thinking this would be the perfect way for me to answer my life's calling: to get people through difficult life changes and on the path to a better life. But I found that most people who are in counseling perpetually live in the Crisis Zone. As a result, therapy tends to have a negative, problem-based orientation. I wanted to take a more positive and proactive approach. My goal was to encourage people to live *quality, purposeful* lives, not just to help them survive at a basic level.

My passion was fueled by this burning thought: *Life is short, life is precious, make the most out of it — make good decisions and choices and make a difference.*

So I left counseling and found a job with Juran Institute, a consulting firm to major corporations aspiring to improve. I became, in essence, a psychologist to businesses. And to my surprise, it was there — in corporate America! — that I discovered the methodology I'd been searching for. Just as I found that I was able to apply lessons from therapy to businesses — in helping people communicate better, develop a stronger rapport with their coworkers, and adapt to change — I found that I could apply lessons from business to individuals.

I quickly realized that the same concepts we were teaching companies for effectively managing their organizations — strategic planning, change management, empowerment, continuous improvement, and customer focus, among others — worked for people looking to effectively manage their personal lives. The good habits of successful companies made sense at the individual level. It seemed so obvious to me that I couldn't believe someone hadn't come up with it before. I started conducting corporate training sessions on the topic at companies like Starbucks and IBM. People who attended my seminars would contact me later to tell me how they'd used the techniques I'd taught them to solve problems in their relationships; manage their debt; further their careers; become more organized; plan for weddings, moves or other major life changes; and so on. *This* was the obvious way for me to accomplish my life goals: I was enabling people to realize positive change and lead the exceptional lives they'd always wanted to live.

In 1992, a professor friend of mine who was familiar with my work, Jim Stoner, asked me to teach a course on using business principles to improve total quality of life at the Fordham University Graduate School of Business in New York City. I accepted. Ever since, I've been working with students to help them develop and implement Exceptional Living Plans. The course has become extremely popular — so much so that I occasionally have to turn people away. It's also helped me fine-tune my methodology, to make it as effective as it can be.

In the past few years, I've expanded my consulting work to serve as a life strategy coach to individuals who want to reach their Purpose Zones. I help them regain balance, manage periods of transition, and envision and achieve goals far beyond any they'd initially even dreamed of pursuing.

My most successful clients and students tell me that they continue to use the techniques they learned from me to this day. They pull out their Exceptional Living Plans every six months to remind themselves of their top priorities, review their progress, and set new goals. And they all feel that they are leading more fulfilling, purpose-driven lives as a result. Their enthusiasm is what convinced me that I needed to share the simple, effective tools provided in this book — which enable you to move from an average to an exceptional life — with others.

Is *Me, Inc.* for You?

There is a new trend in America — a growing recognition of the overlap between what used to be considered strictly business and strictly personal. Why do you think we are so fond of the reality TV show *The Apprentice*, which tests its charming, witty contestants with actual business tasks? I believe it's because we all work or have worked at some point in our lives. We're all familiar with the stress of a last-minute deadline, the elaborate politics of working within a team, and the agony of letting down the big boss. And every single one of us has been a customer. So we can all understand what it means to treat the most important

people in our life as our customers: Taking time to understand and deliver on their needs, or suffering the consequences of not meeting those needs.

Me, Inc. is a book designed to help people manage
transition and optimize their lives, but it draws on the best
practices from the corporate world. It isn't afraid to say,
"You know what? We could all learn some lessons from
the way successful companies operate. Sometimes business does it right."

Me, Inc. gets results because it is based on your own
values and dreams: It's all about figuring out what *you*
want. But it doesn't just stop at that. It also links planning
with execution. Without an implementation strategy, it's
unlikely that you'll make significant changes. Be honest:
How often do you actually follow through on your New
Year's resolutions? This book will show you how to set
meaningful goals *and* put a plan in place for achieving
them. Like the most effective weight loss books, *Me, Inc.*
has a very specific phase-and-step program to follow to
success.

Simply put, *Me, Inc.* is for people who want more out
of life than just a paycheck. It's for anyone who wants to
take control, achieve greater balance, figure out a higher
purpose, and realize their goals. It will resonate especially
well with you if you are:

- A professional who has been exposed in the workplace
  to such business concepts as writing a vision statement,

setting short-term and long-term goals, creating an implementation plan, empowering employees, satisfying customers, and reviewing performance. *Me, Inc.* will teach you how to apply those principles to your personal life.

- In the midst of a major life transition in terms of career, marriage, or child rearing (e.g., graduating from college, becoming a new parent, moving, getting divorced, or starting a new job) and want to find balance. *Me, Inc.* will help you regain control over your chaotic life.

- An aging boomer who will be soon facing retirement and whose children have left home. *Me, Inc.* can guide you in your search for a new purpose in life.

- A high-achievement individual who is motivated to accomplish more. *Me, Inc.* will provide you with the right tools to help you get it all done.

- One of the current wave of workers who are switching to entirely new careers because they have been displaced due to corporate downsizing, restructuring, or mergers, or simply because they want jobs that offer a greater sense of meaning and purpose. *Me, Inc.* can assist you in figuring out what you want to do next and how to get there.

- A fan of self-help books. In this case, you will instantly recognize that *Me, Inc.* offers a refreshing approach for moving to the life you want — one that makes sense because in the end it leaves you with a *personalized action plan*, not just a bunch of talk.

How *Me, Inc.* Works

Me, Inc. will help you find balance, reach new levels of achievement, and discover the satisfaction you've been pining for in your work and personal life. Here's how.

Me, Inc. leads you through 12 milestones to create and implement a concrete plan for achieving your life goals in just 16 weeks. It's not about making little resolutions; it's about implementing a major lifestyle change. Your Exceptional Living Plan will be:

- *Personal.* This is *your* plan for your life, not mine or anyone else's.
- *Applicable.* You can use this plan in all aspects of your life — from your job, to your personal relationships, to your finances, to your physical and spiritual needs — not just one piece of it.
- *Focused.* This plan is specific and factual because it relies on business practices to help you fix what's broken and reach new heights in your life.
- *Practical and doable.* This process makes sense and can be done by anyone — it's not abstract or theoretical. You're left with a concrete action plan laying out specific steps and a timeline for how to move forward.
- *Dynamic.* By the time you finish the book, your Exceptional Living Plan won't be fully executed, but you will already have begun implementing it. You'll be solidly on your way to achieving your life goals.
- *Ongoing.* Your Exceptional Living Plan is a living, breathing document. Even after you've completed

your initial goals, you'll keep updating, changing, and managing your life according to it. After all, your life doesn't end when the book ends.

This four-phase, 16-week plan unfolds logically, leading you to a happier, more purposeful existence:

- In Phase One, you'll take a deep look at your life to determine what your core values and big-picture goals are. You'll ask yourself important questions such as "What is driving my commitment to change my life?" and "Who do I *really* want to be?"
- In Phase Two, you'll determine and rank your priorities, such as healthy relationships, productive career, good physical health, and spiritual well-being. You'll also determine who your "key customers" are. Your "customers" are the people in your life who matter most to you. I use this term because I like the way that businesses always put the customer first, and I feel that exceptional individuals should do the same. Once you've accomplished these milestones, you'll be ready to set both short-term and long-term goals for improving your life and your relationships with your customers. Then, you'll put together an action plan for achieving those goals — your Exceptional Living Plan.
- In Phase Three, you'll begin implementing your Exceptional Living Plan. Using business tools such as data analysis, the Five Why's, and outsourcing, you'll identify and remove barriers to improvement; learn how to exceed your customers' expectations and em-

power them to reach their full potential; and work toward attaining even your loftiest goals.

- Finally, in Phase Four, you'll take responsibility for maintaining a program of continuous improvement. You'll make a lasting commitment to yourself and your loved ones to strive to be the best person you can be. Your life will be better, your relationships stronger, and you'll be living in accordance with your values. You'll have saved yourself from mediocrity.

Note on the Activities

In each chapter of *Me, Inc.* you'll find a concrete exercise to complete that is designed to help you create and implement your Exceptional Living Plan. You'll be writing down your answers to questions, ranking your priorities, brainstorming, setting goals, giving quizzes to your friends and family members, and evaluating your performance over time.

I strongly encourage you not to skip these activities, as they are crucial to helping you move from dreams to reality. Some of the exercises will take just 15 minutes, but others are more involved tasks that may require up to two weeks for you to finish. The number of weeks set aside for each milestone in the book will give you some indication of how much time I usually find it takes my clients and students to move forward to the next step. If you can't follow the timeline precisely, don't panic. Feel free to take as much time as you need. It's more important for you to feel that you have thought things through and created meaningful goals for yourself than it is for you to rush through the book in order to meet some artificial deadline. Remember, the goal is for you to be living the life *you* want to lead. You're in charge!

When you're ready to start an activity, set aside some quiet time for yourself to focus on it without distraction. You can sit down with a pen and paper, or you can work on your computer, as most of my clients and students prefer to do. That way you can edit more easily, copy and paste, and, if you're so inclined, even use the graphing function of Excel. The crucial point is that you write things down and store them in a safe place so that you can review your initial evaluations of your life and track your progress over time.

In the end, you'll have a personalized, detailed model for continuous improvement — an Exceptional Living Plan in action. You'll be able to take Me, Inc. to a whole new level.

You'll be living in the Purpose Zone.

ACTIVITY: Quality-of-Life Index

The only way companies can determine if their business is growing or drying up is to track their current level of performance. Similarly, in order to measure improvements in your personal life, you need to start by evaluating the health of your life right now.

Fill out this self-assessment questionnaire to come up

with a number representing your current quality of life. Be sure to record your answer either in a notebook or on your computer, and keep it somewhere safe. Later, you'll complete the Quality-of-Life Index again, and you'll want to be able to look back at this initial score so that you can measure your progress since beginning the program.

How satisfied are you with the way you are currently living your life?
For each of the following items, please rate yourself on a scale of 1 to 5 (1 = not at all satisfied, 3 = neutral, 5 = very satisfied).

1. My overall quality of life: _____
2. How I manage my time: _____
3. My daily stress level: _____
4. My daily productivity level: _____
5. My physical health: _____
6. My sense of purpose/direction in life: _____
7. How well I am fulfilling my various roles (e.g., mother/father, husband/wife, son/daughter, employee, friend): _____
8. How successfully I am attaining my career goals: _____
9. How well I am adding value to my community: _____
10. How much effort I devote to self-improvement: _____

Add up your numbers for a total Quality-of-Life score (between 10 and 50): _____

If you scored between 10 and 25, this means that you're living primarily in the **Crisis Zone.** You probably feel as though your life is spinning out of control. Don't worry. The methods you'll find in these pages will help put out the fires and reclaim your role as active manager of your life.

If you scored between 26 and 40, then you're living in the **Complacency Zone.** You may think that everything is going relatively smoothly, but chances are there's trouble brewing not far beneath the surface. You've got to engage now if you want to reach your full potential and find greater life satisfaction down the road.

If you scored between 41 and 50, you're living in the **Purpose Zone.** This is where you want to be. Congratulations, you're a good CEO already! But there's always room for improvement. I'm sure you can think of new skills you'd like to develop, people whose needs you could be doing a better job of meeting, and far-reaching goals that you'd like to achieve.

No matter what your score, this book will help you raise it by creating and implementing a plan for getting the life you've always dreamed of having. Now let's get down to the business of living.

Phase I

Figuring Out What You Want and Why You Want It

Self-improvement requires a deep, full commitment. It's not enough to simply think about how nice it would be for your life to get better — you have to internalize the need for change. This starts with recognizing your personal internal motivators for change, and then establishing ownership of them. Commitment also requires that you're up for the challenge and feel mentally prepared, which you must be if you bought and started reading this book in the first place!

So, how on earth are you going to go about it? Just follow the simple steps provided in this book. With each milestone you accomplish, you'll be moving closer and closer to your exceptional life.

In this initial two-week phase, you'll determine why you want to change the way you're currently living and you'll envision how you'd ideally like to live in the (very near!) future.

The Burning Platform

Making a Case for Change

Rose, a 61-year-old divorcée, feels like she's lost her identity. She spent most of her adult life raising her two kids, supporting her husband in his career, and working for the same company. But her kids have graduated from college and have their own families in different cities now. She separated from her husband two years ago, so she's living on her own. And very soon, Rose will be retiring.

Without a job or a family to take care of, Rose has faced the realization that she doesn't know who she is or what she wants to do with her time. "For all those years, I put my own life on hold," she tells me. "I want to rediscover my identity. I haven't really been 'me' since college!" Rose feels that unless she formulates a life plan now, she'll be completely lost when her career comes to an end. She wants an Exceptional Living Plan to help her figure out her new life — what sort of volunteer work she should plan to do after retirement and how to meet new people, including interesting single men.

In a sense, Rose is lucky. There's no question that the transition period she's going through right now is stressful. But on the other hand, she clearly understands the need for developing a plan that will enable her to start leading her life on purpose. Between her recent divorce and her impending retirement, the reasons are clear: If she doesn't take action soon, she'll wind up living in the Crisis Zone. Rose has a strong *case for change.*

Change is a fact of life; there's no such thing as a static state of being. We must face two fundamental types of change—gradual and monumental. We all experience gradual change on a more or less routine basis. For the most part, we're okay with that. We view it as an expected phenomenon as we pass through the various stages of life. It's the monumental change that tends to generate real fear and anxiety.

Take a moment and think back to a time in your life when you made a conscious change in your life. What was the change? What was going on at the time? Did it involve dramatic changes in your lifestyle? Minor changes? Or was it somewhere in between? We all change in different ways, at different stages in our lives, and for different reasons. To better understand the role of change as you try to improve the quality of your life, think of a recent project or goal that you set out to achieve. Whether formally or informally, you most likely first sat down to assess the task. You might have asked yourself some of the following questions:

- What am I trying to accomplish?
- What resources will I need to complete the task?

- What changes to my lifestyle will I have to make?
- Do I have what it takes?
- Will it be worth it in the long run?

In other words, you were making a case for change for yourself. Once you had assessed your competency in completing the task and evaluated its worth, you determined to go forward.

Change is difficult for companies and for individuals. Most people are content with the safe and predictable status quo. Why change if you don't have to? It's like wearing our favorite shoes, sitting in our favorite chair, or eating the same breakfast meal each day. We like things to be predictable, snug, and comfortable. There's something safe and reassuring with what we already know. It feels good. So unless you understand that you could be happier, more productive, and better balanced in your life, you won't feel motivated to take action to do something about it. You've got to find a cause that really rallies you to kick-start the challenging yet rewarding process of self-improvement.

I call this catalyst for change your **Burning Platform.** It's as though you're standing on a 20-foot tall wooden platform that's on fire. You have to decide quickly whether you're going to try to put out the fire, call for help, or jump. Regardless of what you do, the fire makes you feel the urgent need to take action.

What's your Burning Platform? What is going to be your driving force for change? What's going to get you to make the kind of monumental changes in your habits and daily patterns that are required to live an exceptional life? Are you in the Complacency Zone? the Crisis Zone? Maybe you've realized that your family is frustrated by your lengthy and frequent business trips, or that you're too busy to cultivate friendships, or that you're too tired to eat the heart-healthy diet your doctor has asked you to maintain, or that your work is not fulfilling your need to contribute to the world. Perhaps you are so overweight that you can no longer take the early-morning walks you used to love, or you're suffering from depression or anxiety, or you're just feeling stressed out. Whatever the reasons, let them serve as your motivation to change. Remind yourself that if you're not home more often, your marriage will eventually fall apart; if you don't find the energy to eat healthily, you could have a heart attack; if you don't make time for friends, you'll lose them. If you don't change today, Me, Inc. could go out of business. Now's your chance to act, to take control, and to start leading the exceptional life you've always wanted to lead.

Find your Burning Platform and feel its fire burning a hole in you. Embrace the desire to put that fire out no matter what it takes.

ACTIVITY: Cost of Inefficient Living (COIL)

Here's a tool from business that will help you build your Burning Platform, to make a case for change in your life: calculating your Cost of Inefficient Living (COIL).

Just like people, organizations need motivation to go through the difficult process of changing their businesses. CEOs frequently ask me to help them implement new initiatives intended to improve performance. I tell them they first need to identify their Burning Platform — the reason for change that makes them feel like they've *got* to do something or they're going to burn up! Because unless everyone in the organization — from the CEO to the middle managers to the folks working in the stock room — understands the driving need for change, the initiative won't succeed.

In order to light the fire for change, I like to determine the Cost of Poor Quality. I find that companies are rarely aware of how much waste they're creating in terms of faulty products, dissatisfied customers, and unhappy employees. So I analyze the data — customer complaints, reject rates, cycle time, repairs, scrap, and so on — and determine what it's costing them. I put a dollar amount on their unproductiveness. Trust me, this usually motivates managers to improve the way they're doing business *fast*. Talk about a Burning Platform!

Similarly, I've discovered that in our personal lives, most of us just go through life without thinking about what our laziness, fear, boredom, or complacency are *really* costing us. Calculating our COIL encourages us to consider the losses we're suffering as a consequence of inaction. It can be a real change driver.

Beck Weathers, a Dallas pathologist, nearly lost his life before realizing that he had to make a drastic change to focus on what was really important to him — his family. Beck was not only a dedicated professional in his career but also an avid adventurer, a man who climbed mountains, went off to remote places, and lived life on the edge. Beck worked hard and long on the job, and when he took vacations, he used his time to go on one of his wild adventures. This lifestyle naturally gave him little time to spend with his wife and two children.

Beck's epiphany came on May 10, 1996. In an attempt to climb Mount Everest, Beck became separated from his party. Alone and nearly frozen to death (medically speaking, he was in a hypothermic coma), he deeply questioned the choices that he had made in his life. Beck actually saw his family as if they were standing in front of him. Realizing that he had not said "good-bye" and "I love you" filled him with overwhelming sadness. He realized at that moment that his family meant more to him than any adventure or professional achievement. Even though he lost both hands and most of his nose to frostbite, his will to survive and see his family again kept him alive to make it to safety.

Beck's experience was a blinding flash of light and motivator for change. In a sense, he was forced to calculate his COIL. He realized that his choice to devote all his time to his career and his climbing had almost cost him his family, as his wife was very close to divorcing him. This event changed his life, saved his marriage, and also strengthened his relationship with his children.

Beck, now a popular motivational speaker, was quoted in a newspaper article as saying, "The relentless pursuit of success and goals and ambition had dragged out of life what was most precious." Referring to his injuries, he went on to say, "I traded my hands and my face for my family and I accept that bargain. In the end, all that matters is the people you hold in your heart and those who hold you in theirs."

Think about an area of your life that you've been meaning to improve — your career, your physical health, your spiritual life, or your family relationships. Now go through the list below to determine your Cost of Inefficient Living. Write down your responses in the same notebook or save them in the same computer file as your answers to the Quality-of-Life Index, so that you can refer back to them later and see how much you've improved. Don't worry about attaching dollar amounts in each category, as this would prove too complex an exercise. Instead, think of the overall qualitative toll your current lifestyle is taking in the following areas:

- Financial costs — actual wasted dollars. For example, say you ran out of gas because you forgot to fill your tank — again. How much did you have to pay to have your car towed or take a cab to and from the gas station?
- Opportunity costs (e.g., not meeting new people, being passed over for promotion).
- Lost-time costs (e.g., looking for items you can't find, making people wait for you).
- Relationship costs (e.g., neglect, separation, estrangement, divorce).
- Emotional costs (e.g., depression, anxiety, anger, stress, fatigue).
- Physical costs (e.g., illness, missed work, headaches, stomach problems).

Let's say, for example, that the problem you want to solve is that you don't manage your finances carefully enough, and so you frequently bounce checks. The obvious financial cost is the $25 bounced-check fee. But what about the costs in the other categories: the damage you do to the goodwill of the person who cashed your check; the time it takes you to rectify the problem; the annoyance you cause your partner? These are all part of your COIL.

COIL is like an iceberg: There are a few obvious, visible financial costs at the tip, but there are many more hidden costs lying just beneath the surface of the water. We often neglect these hidden costs completely, and yet hidden costs — like making a loved one angry — can prove to be the most deadly of all. That's why running through the entire checklist is so crucial: You experience the full impact of the whole iceberg. And this iceberg represents everything in your life that you need to change. You've found your Burning Platform. The fire is lit.

Before going on to the next chapter, review the following questions:

- Am I satisfied with the way I am currently living my life?
- Am I prepared to make changes in my life?
- Do I resist change, either incremental or monumental? Why?
- What is my Burning Platform?

- What's my COIL?
- Am I willing to start *actively managing* my life?

If you can answer these questions with insight and enthusiasm, then you're ready to begin.

Milestone 2, Week 2

"I Always Wanted to Be . . ."

Establishing Your Platinum Standard

Now that you've identified your Burning Platform, your catalyst for change, it's time to start thinking about what you want to change *to*. What are you really about? How, ideally, would you like to be living your life? With this milestone, you'll pinpoint the guiding principle by which you'd like to live.

Businesses that have vision statements to guide their decisions are much more decisive, more focused, and more efficient. Johnson & Johnson spent years perfecting every word of its credo to "put people before profits." So when the Tylenol scandal erupted in 1982, it knew exactly what to do: Executives pulled every bottle off the shelves nationwide, even though tainted product had been found in only one region of the United States. As a result, consumers maintained their trust in the organization, and it continued to thrive.

People need vision statements, too. Your vision statement *defines your purpose* and gives meaning to your life.
It answers the questions "Who am I?" and "What does
my exceptional life look like?" Redefining the meaning
of success in life begins with our understanding of our
unique purpose in life. Writing out a vision statement is
therefore not an easy task. It requires deep self-exploration
to get in touch with our higher selves and home in on our
truest desires. The process of discovery becomes as important, if not more important, than the final output. Vision
statements are meaningless unless we invest significant
sweat equity in their creation.

Knowing your purpose has both a philosophical and a
spiritual component. Most of us think following a vision
is a business reserved for religious leaders, mystics, or
philosophers. I believe that we are all spiritual beings and
philosophers. We all wonder about the meaning of life.
We've all walked under the tent of stars and asked ourselves what it's all about.

True purpose is based not on what others think of us or
even what we think of ourselves. It is based on our spiritual
essence. Spiritual essence goes beyond external factors to
far deeper levels of existence. While external manifestations provide us with clues and insights as to who we are,
they do not in and of themselves reveal our true essence
and purpose, which is spiritual in nature.

To understand our purpose we must first have a good
understanding of who we *really* are. Most of us have un-

clear, incomplete, or confused ideas about who we really are because we have allowed others, or our circumstances, to define us.

Discovering purpose is not a destination. Rather, it defines a starting point as well as a direction based on where you are at a given moment. We are seeking *truths* about ourselves. As we progress in our life journey we will learn new truths. That doesn't make the previous ones any less relevant, though. It's a bit like climbing a mountain. I remember my first time hiking in the Swiss Alps. I looked up from the base of a particular mountain I had decided to scale and set my sights on its peak—my destination. But as I climbed higher and seemingly nearer to my destination, I discovered that the "peak" was actually nothing more than one of many smaller peaks. So I recalibrated and continued on my journey. When I finally reached the summit, I was awestruck by the panoramic view. I was thrilled to have reached my destination. Yet, as I looked out over the vastness, I thought to myself, "I'll enjoy this view for today. But tomorrow, I'll set out for new heights."

You may be wondering why we're moving into a spiritual realm. You might ask, "Isn't this self-improvement program based on an organizational model of excellence? If so, why are we talking about spirituality?" That's a valid point. But here's the kicker: Even *organizational* improvement is spiritual in essence. Now I'm not talking about religion here; it's not the same thing as spirituality.

At its core, companies' being "spiritual" means they are concerned with doing the right thing, including being socially responsible, delivering value to the customer, providing benefits to the community, being respectful of the environment, and treating employees with dignity and compassion. Former Motorola CEO Robert Galvin went so far as to say that a company leader should love his employees.

Keep in mind that organizations are not just impersonal clumps of bricks and mortar. All organizations were founded by human beings — real people who in many cases were not just out to make a buck; they wanted to change the world. They started with a dream and turned their visions into successful companies. Anita Roddick, for example, created the Body Shop as an extension of her personal style and convictions: protecting the environment and fighting for human rights. Founders often make a lasting imprint on the values and culture of that organization. And what's more, all the companies ranked as "great," "most admired," and "best places to work" have a spiritual underpinning.

But even companies can make the mistake of defining themselves by external manifestations. As a marketing student in college, I recall a professor sharing a fascinating story about how the Bic company changed its business by changing the way it thought of itself. As the story was told to me, Bic retained a marketing consultant to provide assistance on expanding its product line and opening up new markets. The company's only product at the time was the Bic pen. The pen was a cash cow, but executives weren't sure how long sales could be maintained. After lengthy research, the consultant made the following recommendation: "Make razors."

The Bic executives were incredulous: "Razors? What a crazy idea! We manufacture pens. What do razors have to do with pens?" The consultant explained that Bic had defined its business by what it made versus what the business was really all about. Its vision of itself was way too narrow. It saw itself as a company that made writing instruments, when in fact its true essence — as the consultant had discovered — was really producing lightweight, inexpensive, disposable plastic consumer products. This revelation opened up a whole new world to the company. With their new understanding, employees quickly thought up other expressions of Bic's true essence. The company had a great deal of success with razors, as the consultant suggested, as well as with lighters. All of this came about because the consultant asked the fundamental question "What is Bic really all about?"

This concept has tremendous implications when applied to our personal lives. To come to grips with our purpose, we must first have a good understanding of who we really are. Most of us have unclear, incomplete, or confused ideas on the subject because we have allowed others or our circumstances to define us. We choose mates, careers, friends, and activities based on an often limited sense of who we are. Many of us view our purpose in terms of our relationships to other people. You hear this in the mother who says, "I live for my kids," or the love-struck adolescent who exclaims, "I'm nothing without you!" Often, we base our image of ourselves on associations, status, wealth, possessions, activities, accomplishments, club memberships, unique physical and intellectual capabilities, and so on. But there's great danger in defining ourselves by such external factors because if and when we lose one of them, we lose our identity. Some people define themselves so narrowly that if any one aspect of their external image goes away (job, marriage), their sense of self-worth is destroyed or greatly weakened. This is why it is so critical that we look deeper to discover our true nature and base our life goals upon these realizations.

Years ago during the American League national championship series between the New York Yankees and the Seattle Mariners, I had a chance meeting with Yankee baseball great Don Mattingly. He was waiting outside the tunnel to the stadium field in preparation for throwing the first pitch. I thought to myself, if anyone defined him- or herself by a single role, it would be a professional athlete, especially someone like Don Mattingly (a.k.a. "Donnie Baseball"). He was obsessed with baseball — or so I thought. Seeing him standing there alone, I decided to question him about his chosen career, and also try to find out why he had announced his retirement when many, including myself, thought he had some great playing years ahead of him. His answer surprised me. "I've always loved baseball and played the game well," he said, "but I never let it define me. I'm a husband and a father. I wanted to spend time with my kids while they're still young. I also have many other interests besides baseball, such as show horses." I said, "But won't you miss the game, the fans, the excitement?" He replied simply, "No. Not even a little bit. I really enjoy my family and wouldn't change a thing." He seemed extremely sincere. He apparently was very aware of his total self, and clearly had not defined himself in too narrow a sense. Today, with his kids grown, he has returned to the game as batting coach for the New York Yankees.

When Rose, the 61-year-old divorcée from the previous chapter, who would be retiring soon, first approached me, I told her she needed to start by writing her vision statement. At first she had no idea what I meant. We discussed it further, and I showed her many examples from my clients and students. Eventually, she decided that the only way she would be able to come up with a vision statement would be to go on a retreat. So she spent a long weekend at a meditation and yoga center in the countryside. After this investment of time and energy in soul-searching, here are some of the things Rose came up with: "I'm looking forward to retirement, but I need to stay busy. It'll drive me crazy to be around the house all the time! I need to feel useful, like I'm making a difference in the world." We refined her words a bit over time, but even in their rough form you can imagine how critical these statements were to our process. In defining what mattered most to Rose, we were able to figure out how she should focus her efforts going forward. How else would we have known that finding a stimulating and meaningful volunteer opportunity should be her top priority rather than, say, exercising or going on vacation more often?

I like to call vision statements, whether they apply to businesses or individuals, **Platinum Standards.** Why? Because in Washington, D.C., within the walls of the National Bureau of Standards, there exists a one-meter length of platinum that is considered to be the most perfect measure of a meter. Platinum has unique qualities: It doesn't rust, corrode, shrink, expand, or break down in any way. In terms of your life vision, having a "Platinum" Standard suggests that some things are nonnegotiable. *Your Platinum Standard doesn't change, no matter what challenges you face in life.* It is what all your other decisions and actions are based upon. It is your moral compass. A Platinum Standard is characterized by the following qualities:

- It provides us with a crystal-clear understanding of our purpose and/or cause.
- It requires unwavering commitment by the "leader"— in this case YOU!
- It integrates all facets of life.
- It considers our value system (core values, beliefs, and guiding principles).

Ultimately, we must behave in a manner that is consistent and congruent with our Platinum Standard.

You should aim for your Platinum Standard to be

- *Multidimensional versus singly focused.* Try to create a statement that encompasses all aspects of your life — not just career, family, or physical health. Put your thoughts in more general terms so that they truly embody your spiritual essence. An all-inclusive Platinum Standard leads to a well-rounded life.
- *Qualitative versus quantitative.* Remember, it's not how much you have; it's how well you are living your life. We will get down to nitty-gritty quantitative measures later (I promise!). For your Platinum Standard, use descriptive, qualitative words.
- *Selfless versus selfish.* Your Platinum Standard should include not only what you do for yourself, but also what you do for your loved ones and others whose lives intersect with yours. An outward-focused existence is more satisfying than an inward-focused one.
- *Motivating.* Working toward a Platinum Standard is in itself a motivator. Your vision statement should inspire you by igniting a fire within the depths of your soul.
- *Positive.* Your Platinum Standard should ignore current obstacles and perceived limitations. Vision statements can be stifled by negativism. You may think, "I haven't the intelligence, the strength, or the moral fortitude to accomplish all that I want." Granted, we have

limitations. But it's by creating goals and reaching for the highest standards that we become determined to overcome them.

- *Enduring.* Your Platinum Standard should not change even as your specific goals in life do. It is a lasting statement about who you are and what you want out of life. Yes, it's true that you and the world at large are in a constant state of flux. You need to expect change and learn to flow with it. At the same time, the reason you're writing your Platinum Standard in the first place is so that you can always refer back to it and use it to ground you, no matter how crazy things get. Try to maintain your focus on the big picture as you write, and create a statement that will last.

Steve wrote this Platinum Standard:

"To be a healthy and happy person. To lead my life with utmost integrity and passion. To be patient with everyone (including myself). To recognize people's strengths and talents. To achieve balance between my personal and professional life. To live life in the present, here and now."

Another client of mine wrote quite simply:

"To be the best I can be every day, and in doing so, to make richer the lives of those around me."

And yet one more:

"To be content. Not rich, not poor, but simply content. I yearn to look around, chuckle to myself, and know that I deliberately chose the path upon which I stand. Take my life's achievements, disappointments, mistakes, triumphs, secrets and proclamations and internally accept my standing and fate in life."

So, how do you go about this intense process of self-discovery? Here's an activity that I find extremely useful in helping my clients and students to establish and record their Platinum Standards.

ACTIVITY: The Big Dig

For over a decade, Boston has been tearing up the very heart of its own city in order to solve its horrendous traffic problem. As one of the largest, most technically difficult infrastructure projects ever undertaken in U.S. history, the Big Dig has been no piece of cake — it has disrupted everyday life for millions of people. But the anticipated benefits are great: improved traffic flow, reduced accidents, less pollution, and more open space.

Establishing your Platinum Standard is a lot like the Big Dig. It requires not just a superficial scraping at the surface, but rather an in-depth probing into the core of who you are and what you want out of life. This is really the key to establishing a Platinum Standard as opposed to just throwing together a vision statement: It's not about the words you put down on paper, it's about the process you use to get there. There are many ways you can choose to get in touch with your higher self. In the classes that I teach, I encourage my students to read books, conduct interviews with people they admire, and even go on retreats in order to come up with their Platinum Standards. You could also take a trip to the wilderness, or spend time discussing the topic with your loved ones or a spiritual leader.

The Big Dig is no easy task. Often, when you dig deep enough, you come across some old skeletons buried in the dirt. But the more you put into this exercise, the more you'll get out of it. Your hard work will pay off with a new and improved you.

Begin your Big Dig by asking yourself two fundamental questions: "Who am I?" and "What matters most to me?" Sketch out your initial ideas on a piece of paper. Don't worry about the specific language. Remember to consider all aspects of your life — career, family, friends, personal well-being, and so on. Now take your early draft and share it with a few people who know you well and whose opinions you trust and respect — partner, spiritual counselor, close friend, or the like. Ask them for their feedback. Compare what you wrote and what others said, and try to find commonalities. Now try writing it again. Make your Platinum Standard positive and motivating.

Here are some questions you can ask yourself to help flesh out your Platinum Standard:

How you see yourself:
- How do you introduce yourself when meeting new people?

- If you wrote a personal ad, what would it say?
- What's your family life like?
- What are your hobbies and interests?
- What kinds of books do you read? What music do you listen to? What movies do you enjoy?
- If you could be anything at all, what would you be?
- What would you have written on your tombstone?

How others see you:

- How do your close friends and family describe you?
- What do coworkers say about you?
- What kind of feedback are you given at performance reviews at work?
- What would people say about you at your funeral?

Once you've compiled a reasonably complete list, review it and see if you can find some common denominators, as in the Bic pen example. For instance, when I decided to leave my first job — as a consultant with Juran Institute — I spent time seriously pondering what I might do next. At first, it was difficult to see myself as anything but a quality management consultant, which is what I had spent 11 years doing. That's how I defined myself. But I wanted something different — a new experience and greater challenges.

Using my resume as a guide, I started asking myself, "Who am I really?" I wanted to look past the title. What specifically was it about being a consultant that I liked? Perhaps the consultant label was the same as Bic's identification of itself as a manufacturer of writing instruments. A deeper dive revealed, for instance, that consultants are problem solvers. I liked the challenge of figuring things out, but discovered that the real fulfillment lay in the fact that I was *helping* people. I also liked the rewards and recognition, the freedom and entrepreneurial aspects of the consulting life. In addition, my job responsibilities included training and public speaking, which indicated that I enjoyed being "on stage." It was a way to scratch the acting itch I've always had, but it was also a way to facilitate learning. I liked the immediate feedback, too. When you're up in front of a group of people you generally have a pretty good sense of how well you're doing: applause, laughter, facial expressions, alertness level (anyone snoozing?). Immediate feedback is important to me because it tells me if I am on the right track and making a positive contribution. I examined extracurricular activities as well. I was a part-time disc jockey on a local FM radio station. Being live on the radio required quick thinking and wit, which I found challenging and fun.

On the surface, there doesn't appear to be a connection between the many, seemingly disparate aspects of our lives. That's because they are manifestations of spiritual essence. But here are some common threads I discovered in my own activities:

helping people
solving problems
seeing results
receiving recognition
being active
taking on challenges

This awareness helped me to think outside the box in my career search. Instead of seeking the obvious consulting opportunities, I broadened my horizons. I ended up creating a position that did not exist prior to my arrival with Peale Center, a nonprofit magazine publisher. The position involved the creation of new services and offerings designed to improve people's lives — exactly what I'd decided was important to me. Aside from my career, I found other ways to pursue my interests: writing books, mentoring, and beginning my work as a life strategy coach.

I believe that our deepest subconscious motivator is the drive for meaning and purpose in life. To be truly happy, you need a clear sense of direction. You need a commitment to something higher than yourself. You need to feel that your life stands for something, that you are making a valuable contribution. Happiness can be defined as the progressive realization of a worthy ideal. Pursuing happiness for its own sake leaves one feeling empty and useless. According to a recent article on the subject in *The New York Times,*

> Some psychologists dispute the choice of happiness itself as an index of the good life. "Satisfaction is a byproduct of a life that involves more than the mere pursuit of happiness," said Dr. Carol Ryff, a developmental psychologist at the University of Wisconsin. "I would argue that it's worse to wake up

in the morning without having a larger purpose in life than to wake up unhappy. Just feeling good is a poor measure of the quality of one's life."

You can only be happy, in the truest sense of the word, when you are working toward a broad vision that is very important to you. Your Platinum Standard is the foundation for your life, so take your time getting it right.

Phase II

Creating Your Exceptional Living Plan

Okay, so now you know your purpose — you've figured out why *you want to change and, on a grand scale, what* you *want to become. Next you've got to figure out* how *you're going to do it.*

Although having a Burning Platform and a Platinum Standard are important and necessary steps, they're not enough. Many people have visions for what they want their lives to become. But without specific plans for translating vision statements into reality, people are not energized or directed by them, and often end up abandoning them.

This is a common phenomenon in organizations. As a consultant I have reviewed hundreds of vision statements, and I've found that overall, if you've read one, you've read them all. Companies will often default to existing templates or copy from others. After all, why reinvent the wheel? Teams are assembled to wordsmith the document. Many organizations spend enormous amounts of time and energy debating the semantics of

the vision statement, going through iteration after iter-
ation. Once agreed upon (usually by committee) and
approved by a senior executive (who more than likely
was not involved early in the process), the statements
are printed. And then the company begins to see mas-
sive improvements, right? Wrong! The vision state-
ments are distributed, placed in prominent spots
throughout the organization such as marketing bro-
chures, web sites, and annual reports, and promptly
forgotten. For example, how many times have you read
vision statements that say, "Our most important asset
is our people," from companies that don't invest in
training, educating, and developing people because
it's too expensive?

The following comes directly from a particular com-
pany's vision statement, as published in its annual re-
port a few years back. See if you can guess whose it is.

Respect: *We treat others as we would like to be*
treated ourselves. We do not tolerate abusive or dis-
respectful treatment. Ruthlessness, callousness, and
arrogance don't belong here.

Integrity: *We work with customers and prospects*
openly, honestly, and sincerely. When we say we will
do something, we will do it; when we say we cannot
or will not do something, then we won't do it.

If you've guessed Enron, then you're correct. The
words are terrific, and the intent behind them is great.

Yet the words and intent did not match the actions at the leadership level.

Don't be like a poor-performing organization and set your Platinum Standard aside. Instead, translate it into actual terms that will start to influence your daily life. The key to success is good planning. In this four-week phase, I'll help you create your Exceptional Living Plan. We'll begin at the highest level and gradually work our way down to the specific details.

What Matters Most

Getting Your Priorities Straight

The fact that you've established your Platinum Standard is impressive. It serves as a beacon to guide you in the direction of your exceptional life. But it certainly doesn't illuminate the exact path you can follow to get there. It's time to start drawing yourself a map.

Organizations know the areas of their business that they absolutely must manage well in order to succeed. These consist of both quantitative (e.g., earnings, revenue, profit margin, stock price) and qualitative measures (e.g., customer loyalty, employee satisfaction, complaints, rework). Similarly, in your personal life you need to start getting specific about creating a life plan by figuring out what your top priorities are.

We often talk about the importance of work-life balance. Generally, what people mean by this is that they're trying to find a way to juggle their job responsibilities while maintaining a satisfying personal life. This is an oversimplification. Life is far more complex. Rather than seeking to attain some unachievable state of perfect balance that we somehow imagine will endure life's constant ups and downs, we should instead focus our efforts on being effective managers of our total lives. As we have discussed before, managing involves setting priorities, solving problems, making decisions, establishing trade-offs, taking risks, allocating resources, and negotiating, to name just a few responsibilities. It's time to determine where you are going to concentrate your efforts.

Ask yourself, "What general areas of my life must I absolutely manage well in order to succeed in manifesting my Platinum Standard?" Creating categories will help you break your overall vision into smaller, more manageable pieces.

Here is a list of the seven key factors that I consider critical to a well-lived life:

1. Solid interpersonal relationships
2. Physical health
3. Spiritual fulfillment
4. Emotional well-being
5. Intellectual stimulation
6. Career achievement
7. Financial security

Think of these categories as instruments on the dashboard of your car. You keep track of each gauge's reading to ensure a safe, reliable journey. There are neither too few nor too many for you to get a sense of how well your car is doing with one quick glance. Each instrument measures something different — fuel level, temperature, speed — but all are critical in getting you to your destination.

You may have other categories, or "instruments," such as hobbies, philanthropy, or miscellaneous, that you want to add to your control panel. Don't feel limited by the ones I've written here. Remember, this is *your* life you're planning, not anyone else's. Write your list down in your notebook or computer file, and save it along with the results to your Quality-of-Life Index, COIL, Burning Platform, and Platinum Standard. Don't worry right now about putting the categories in any particular order; you'll be doing that later.

I have a friend, Kris, who is a stay-at-home mom. She's found this role extremely fulfilling. But her son, who is four, will be starting school full time next year, and Kris is freaking out about what to do with her time when he does. Even though her husband can afford to support the family, she doesn't think she'll be content to remain a home-maker forever. Being a smart, well-educated, outgoing woman, Kris has plenty of options — so many, in fact, that she feels overwhelmed. Should she go back to working as an attorney, as she did before she had her son? Should she open a T-shirt shop? Start a catering business?

In order to help her make a decision, I suggested that Kris first determine her Platinum Standard, then list and rank her priorities. Family came first, then gaining personal satisfaction through a job, then health and friends. Making money came last. As soon as she looked at her list,

Kris felt that her choice was clear. In order to remain available to her husband and son, she should only seek a part-time job. That ruled out the possibility of going back to her law firm, where 80-hour weeks were standard. The T-shirt shop had greater earning potential, but the catering business appealed to her more on a personal level because she has always loved cooking and thought she could get a friend to start the business with her.

Once she'd examined her priorities, Kris was quickly able to home in on the option that made the most sense for her. Now it's time for you to do that, too. I'm going to talk in a bit more depth here about each of the seven categories that I see as critical to leading an exceptional life.

Spiritual Fulfillment

Most people have some sense of spirituality. If this includes you, I suggest that it may be your most important priority. Think of it as a centering power or anchor that forms the foundation of all your other activities in life. The logic behind this notion is "Do this first, and do it well, and the rest will fall naturally into place." Interestingly enough, I find that most of my clients and students do rank spirituality number one, but only in principle. In actuality, it usually falls to the bottom of their list.

I view spirituality and religion as slightly different, yet connected. I was brought up Roman Catholic. Although I was religious in that I followed the practices, doctrines, and dogma of the church as a child, I don't think I was par-

ticularly spiritual. Over time, I focused more on my spirituality through meditation, contemplation, prayer, and
simply being out in nature. Something very interesting
happened as a result: My spiritual quest gave me a much
deeper understanding of my particular faith. Instead of
just showing up and going through the motions at church,
I felt a meaningful connection with my beliefs. Up until
that time, I had never experienced the feeling that my religious faith was my own. Instead, it was something that
was imposed on me. I do not fault my parents; they were
doing the right thing in raising me in their faith. But at
some point we need to make our own conscious, unbi-
ased, informed choices. What I perceive as my spirituality
strengthens my faith, which in turn has made me more
spiritual or inward looking. The two seem to feed off of
one another.

In our busy modern lives, we often allow both spirituality and religion to drop right off our instrument panels.
There are many reasons for this. For starters, compared
with our careers, there are few immediate rewards or consequences if we aren't diligent about our faith. In our jobs,
we receive regular paychecks and ongoing performance
appraisals. But spirituality and religion are intangible. We
can't see, touch, or smell the results of our efforts in a concrete way, so we more easily lose sight of the benefits. Yet
if we neglect our spiritual lives, they deteriorate. As a result
we lose the anchor in our lives.

Actively attending to our spirituality is like taking pre-
ventive medicine: It keeps us healthy whether we con-

sciously know it or not. We focus more on our responsibilities to ourselves and our loved ones because we see and feel our *connectedness* to each other. We're more aware of our physical needs and less inclined to abuse our bodies through excessive drinking, eating, smoking, or lack of exercise. We tend to stay more focused on the big picture in life, remembering that all our actions, both positive and negative, have an impact and universal consequences.

Only you can decide what spirituality means to you. Once you do, you can begin incorporating it into your life by setting some strategic goals. For example, you might decide to attend church or temple services; meditate; go on retreats; pray; volunteer to work with the poor, homeless, or sick; spend time in nature; or read inspirational literature. There's enough here to stimulate your thinking.

Solid Interpersonal Relationships

Life involves a series of interactions with other human beings. Some relationships are simple, others very complex. Some are professional (with bosses, employees, coworkers), and others are personal (with parents, spouse, children, friends, spiritual leaders). But we must effectively manage all of them. Imagine trying to achieve your goals or live out your vision without involving other people! At a later stage in this process, you'll identify your most important personal relationships. For now, just think about how your quality of life is impacted if you ignore certain relationships.

Physical Health

Generally speaking, we have got to take better care of our bodies. Obesity rates are on the rise, in spite of the incredible advances we've made in creating healthier foods, better medicine and surgery techniques, and advanced exercise equipment and accessories. I don't think we need experts to provide us with the answers, either. I've found that in today's culture we look for quick fixes like special drugs, treatments, or food additives. And yet while the latest fads in nutrition and exercise constantly change, the basic rules remain the same: We are what we eat and do. It's all very commonsense. If you want to lose weight, feel great, and enjoy long-term health benefits, then exercise more and consume more fruits and vegetables and fewer fatty, processed foods. Avoid smoking, and don't drink heavily. It's as simple as that. All that most of us need is greater discipline and better habits. Commit to and follow through with whatever health regimen appeals the most to you.

I made a commitment to a healthy lifestyle when I was in high school because for most of my life my father was sick. He was a heavy smoker, was overweight, and suffered from heart disease and diabetes. Although genetic factors that are out of our control definitely play a role in health, I realized that I could take control of my own health habits to avoid a similar fate. Ever since, I have exercised regularly, eaten well, and maintained an appropriate weight.

Emotional Well-Being

In our materialistic society, we often get caught up in the misconception that possessions like clothing, jewelry, cars, vacations, and houses are the keys to happiness. I feel that it is possible to derive great satisfaction from pursuing and obtaining such goods. However, we want to avoid being possessed by our possessions — letting what we want or imagine we need for a fulfilling life control our lives and dominate our thinking.

When we accumulate stuff, we have to spend more time caring for it. I remember buying my first sports car, a limited-edition turbo-charged Nissan 300ZX. It was a pleasure to drive. But after a couple of years, I tired of trying to maintain it. I was obsessed with keeping it clean, and would constantly worry that it would get dinged in the parking lot or, worse yet, stolen. As much as I liked it, I sold it and bought a Jeep Wrangler, which is a fun, lower-end, worry-free automobile. Someday I will buy another sports car, but only when I don't have to use it as my primary vehicle.

Are your possessions robbing you of free time or peace of mind? When you set your goals for emotional well-being, keep your material needs and desires in perspective. The time you spend caring for or obsessing over your possessions almost certainly would be better spent gardening, watching the sunset with someone you love, listening to a friend in need, visiting an aging parent, or playing dress-up with your daughter. These are the kinds of activities that you should prioritize in your life in order to enjoy lasting emotional fulfillment.

Intellectual Stimulation

Unless you're in a profession that requires continuous education, chances are, like so many others, you have let learning slip by the wayside. For many of us, focused learning slows down once we've completed our formal education. But if anything, we should be increasing our learning opportunities instead of decreasing them. Science tells us that our brain cells naturally deteriorate as we age but that we can halt this process and even generate new cells with consistent intellectual stimulation.

There are many ways in which you might consider keeping your mind from turning to mush. You could set a goal to reduce the amount of time you spend passively watching television. Use that extra hour to read a book, play a challenging game like chess, complete a crossword puzzle, or even take a continuing education course.

Like me, I'm sure you fall into predictable patterns. I often get into the habit of reading only business books and magazines. But to truly expand our minds, we should try new activities. For instance, over the past year, I set a goal of reading more fiction. As it turned out, my 11-year-old daughter Jennifer was reading the Harry Potter books by J. K. Rowling. Although at first I had no interest in reading a children's book, I thought picking up a Harry Potter book myself would be a great way to bond with my daughter and meet my fiction goal. Well, within the first few pages, I was completely engrossed. Jennifer would always stay one book ahead of me, but we had a lot of fun discussing the characters, plots, and subplots.

We learn and grow especially through new experiences, whether literature, games, places, people, or hobbies. In his autobiography, Winston Churchill extolled the value of having interest in things other than those we depend on for our career. He loved to paint in watercolor. He wrote that painting helped him relax and took him away from the cares of the world. It also re-energized him when he returned to his immense duties and responsibilities.

Career Achievement

"Everybody's working for the weekend," the saying goes. It suggests that the sole purpose of work is to bring home a paycheck so that you can look forward to a weekend of revelry and relaxation. There was a real buzz around my town in Connecticut recently when the multistate lottery reached a record jackpot of over 150 million dollars. "What would you do if you won?" people asked each other. "The first thing I'd do is quit my job," I heard many reply.

I feel that work has gotten a bad rap. Yes, it's true that many people are miserable in their jobs. For some, work is boring and routine. For others, the problem is that they are overworked and stressed out. Still others are frustrated and worn out because of a demanding boss, customer, or coworker. I've found, however, that work itself is typically not the villain. All of us have experienced times when we were fed up with our jobs for whatever reason. But in my experience, deep down most people do not want to live a life of leisure forever, especially if they have enjoyed their careers at some point. Recent research shows that we are living longer than ever before. We all know of people who, once retired, initially went all out enjoying themselves—traveling, spending time with grandchildren, seeing friends, playing golf, and engaging in hobbies and various interests. But after only a year or so, they began to grow restless and got the itch to go back to work, on their own terms. Perhaps they started volunteering or took on a part-time job. But they announced to friends that they couldn't stand being at leisure all the time.

Our jobs are crucial to our well-being. They take up a third or more of our time. If you're in a job that makes you miserable, it will have a huge impact on your overall quality of life. There are many good books on the market about career development, so I won't repeat what I think has already been said. But I would like to offer a perspective that you may find helpful as you consider the age-old question "What do I want to be when I grow up?"

Career satisfaction is based not so much on what we do as *why* we do it. We need to change our mindset about work in general. Whether you're a stay-at-home parent, entrepreneur, laborer, or office worker, you can derive true fulfillment from work by finding meaning in what you do. For instance, I view my multiple professional roles as business consultant, life strategy coach, and professor all as ways of ministering to the needs of others. Can you reframe how you perceive your job, viewing it not as a chore but rather as an expression of who you are and a tool for making an impact on the world?

Financial Security

You may be surprised to hear me say it after all this talk of spirituality and relationships, but yes, even I believe that the accumulation of wealth is necessary for a high-quality life. Achieving a certain degree of financial security eases anxiety and helps us enjoy a full range of what the world has to offer. What's crucial is not letting money become the driving force in our lives.

I have found that many people begin their careers focused on making a valuable contribution to society. Although money is important to them, they often don't care about how big a salary they're earning. But as financial obligations increase, so does our perceived need to make more money. Somewhere along the line, many of us lose perspective. We begin to live beyond our means, creating increased pressure on ourselves to earn more. Earning more requires that we take on greater responsibilities, which often translates into working longer hours, traveling more, and experiencing higher stress levels at work on a daily basis. Before we know it, we find that we are focused exclusively on earning versus doing work that we find enjoyable and challenging.

Part of the solution lies in managing your finances, so

that you keep your expenditures within the limits of your paycheck. Assuming you're not in work crisis mode, there's a simple formula for creating financial security: Save more and spend less (which we as a society don't do). It's exactly like the formula for being healthy: Exercise more and eat less. Once again, all we need is some personal discipline to abide by the commonsense rules.

It's fine to want to advance your career. I'm not suggesting that you abandon your work goals. I'm only suggesting that you shouldn't let your desire for more money (or your fear of not having enough) drive your decision-making process. First, get a handle on your finances. Then, set goals such as reducing spending and debt. Once again, you can find a plethora of books on the subject, but most people don't need sophisticated advice. All you need to do is handle the basics and handle them well!

ACTIVITY: Priority Pyramids

You've determined the broad categories that you feel are critical for leading a purposeful, fulfilling life. Now, let's figure out how important each of them is to achieving your Platinum Standard. Ranking these categories in order of priority may prove challenging, but it's important. In order to make a plan for achieving a more satisfying, balanced, exceptional life, you need to know how you are *actually* living your life in relation to your vision for how you *want* to be living it.

Write down your categories according to how important they are to you. Now write them down again according to how you currently live your life. Seeing the two lists — the ideal versus reality — juxtaposed like this will reveal where the discrepancies lie. These are the areas you'll most need to focus your attention on from this point forward.

Here's an example of what your ideal versus actual Priority Pyramids might look like (areas for improvement are indicated with stars):

Ideal Priority List	*Priority List in Reality*
**Spiritual fulfillment	Career achievement
Solid relationships	Solid relationships
*Emotional well-being	Financial security
*Career achievement	Emotional well-being
Intellectual stimulation	Intellectual stimulation
Physical health	Physical health
*Financial security	Spiritual fulfillment

A student of mine told me about a man in her office who did an exemplary job of keeping his priorities straight:

> I used to work with someone who was in a senior position at the company when his wife gave birth to their second child. Upon returning from paternity leave, he scaled back his schedule to four days a week—three days in the office and one day at home. On the days when he was in the office, he was completely efficient at getting his work done by

5:00 P.M. so that he could leave to pick up his older daughter at day care. On the day he worked from home, he was as accessible and reliable as if he were working in the office. However, on the day when he was not working, he told us to not even think about contacting him. He would not take our calls or answer our e-mails. That was his day to be a dad.

He had his priorities in order, and he stuck by them. And if he worked at a company that didn't respect his priorities, he'd have a Burning Platform — he'd need to change to a job that would enable him to live his life according to his Platinum Standard and priorities.

And now you've got your priorities in order. You're on your way!

Who Matters Most

Incorporating Others into Your Plan

With the first three milestones, you've figured out what you want out of life. Now you need to turn your attention to *others*. After all, our quality of life is determined to a large extent by the quality of our relationships with other people. A life lived on purpose is sel*fless* rather than sel*fish*.

In fact, I find that for most of my students and coaching clients, the "solid interpersonal relationships" category takes the number one or two spot on their ideal Priority Pyramid. They're working on an Exceptional Living Plan not just for themselves, but also so that they can enhance friendships, make more time for loved ones, and be better people. Relationships aren't just *a* priority — they are a *top* priority.

Although it may seem cold and impersonal at first, I find it extremely helpful to think of the key people in our lives as our customers. Why? Because in business, the customer comes first. Companies are always looking for ways to keep their customers loyal by anticipating and even exceeding their needs. Exceptional companies refuse to be satisfied with just "good enough" customer service.

Look at the word *customer*. You'll see that it contains another word: *custom*. The word *customer* literally means "giver of custom." Custom was offered as an honor and a bond of trust. And it was taken away as an act of rejection, which was taken very seriously both by the one who once held custom and by the one who took it away. Think about this transaction for a moment: "Promise quality, and I will give you my 'custom' from which your product and service can be fashioned." Ponder the magnitude of the act of giving and utilizing custom. Does it not represent the most elemental force of business? To give one's custom is to form a bond of business. To take it away is to remove business — for one customer, or many.

Now think about it again. We've all been customers for our entire lives. You know the companies that do it right — they pay attention to your needs, listen to your complaints, and make you feel special, so you go back to them over and over again. You also know when companies do it wrong. Just remember the last time a clerk treated you poorly at a clothing store or coffee shop, for example. You probably haven't been back since.

I often think of the time I was eating at the famous Stage Deli restaurant in New York. As I was finishing the delicious pickle that accompanied my pastrami sandwich, I was thinking to myself, "Gee, I wish I had another." Magically, my waiter appeared at that very moment and delivered an extra pickle to my table. "How did you know?" I asked. "It's my job to figure out what you want before you even realize it yourself," he replied. Ten years later, I still remember his name: Norm.

You should adopt a similar customer service attitude in your personal life. If you consider your loved ones your most prized customers, then you'll treat them well, and they'll treat you well in return. On the other hand, if you don't take your customers' needs and wants seriously, they'll take their "business" elsewhere. The cost of losing customers is high — broken friendships, estrangement, separation, divorce, and so on. You can lose these relationships forever.

A former student of mine, Ashley, does a great job of taking care of her customers. She always aims to deliver exceptional service in order to safeguard their loyalty. For example, in choosing her current career, Ashley says, "Your class helped me realize that being the best daughter and wife I can be was my highest priority." So during the job interview process, she made it clear to her potential employer that she needed to be home by dinnertime every night and wouldn't work weekends. That may seem like quite an audacious condition to you, but it worked wonders for Ashley. Not only did she get the job, but she has also proven a top performer for several years now and has already been promoted. By setting clear expectations and sticking to her priorities, Ashley has kept her family and her boss — her two most important customers, in that order — satisfied.

So let's figure out who your customers are, and who

among them is most important to you. Like businesses, we
have many customers in our personal lives. Some are obvious, others not so obvious. Take a moment now and
brainstorm a list of your customers. Think about the roles
you play in life, as well as the activities you're involved in,
and list all the people you come in contact with on a regular basis. List everybody you can think of — don't leave
anybody out, and be creative. Your list might include the
following:

God/higher spiritual power	Roommate(s)
Self	Boss
Spouse	Coworkers
Significant other	Employees
Children	Landlord
Parents	Fellow citizens
Friends	Commuters
Acquaintances	Public service officials
Relatives	Teachers
	and so on. . .

Compare your list to the people on your holiday card
list — have you forgotten anybody?

ACTIVITY: Circles of Customers

One of my most interesting and challenging consulting
assignments involved a well-known fast food chain headquartered in the Northeast. I was asked to facilitate a pro-

cess improvement project in one of their outlets. During a meeting with management and key staff, I asked the question, "Who are your customers?" An arm quickly shot up from a cashier, who said, "Our customers are the people who come into the store to purchase our product." Then one of the bakers chimed in and said, "The purchaser is not my customer. My customer is the person who prepares the sandwich." Then the person in charge of catering said, "My customer is the individual representing corporations who phones in large catering orders." At this point, everyone began to see that their customers were actually like a cast of characters playing various roles, each one representing a unique set of needs and demands.

Upon closer investigation, the group found that their customers could be broken down into different categories based on their level of importance. For instance, the catering customer was considered to be more valuable than the individual walk-in customer because she placed larger orders. If the vice president of sales hosted a lunch meeting for her sales reps, her receptionist would receive the delivery, the reps would eat the food, and the VP would pay for it. Suddenly the customer list grew from one to four, each one with a different set of needs.

Similarly, meeting your customers' needs in your personal life requires first determining *who* they are and then ranking them in order of priority.

So now go ahead and make a list of all the people who matter in your life — family members, friends, coworkers, community members, and maybe even you. Now that you know who your customers are, prioritize them. Draw three concentric circles (see the illustration for an example). Label the innermost one G for Gold, the middle one S for Silver, and the outermost one B for Bronze. Place your most valued customers in Gold, your second-tier clients in Silver, and your third-tier customers in the Bronze circle.

Ranking people in this way may seem harsh. But we ought to consider that people, like companies, only have limited resources to allocate. Prioritizing is the best way to ensure that you devote the bulk of your time and energy to your most important customers. My students and clients generally find that this exercise makes their relationships simpler and more fulfilling.

For example, have you ever had one of those friends who seems to suck up every bit of yourself that you're willing to share? She's always calling on the phone to tell you about her latest crisis, but never seems to inquire as to how you're doing. Perhaps you should consider cutting back on the amount of time that you spend with this individual. Allocate those precious resources to a beloved family member in the Gold circle instead, or use them to take care of your own needs.

Do you take better care of your customers than you do of yourself? This is not a selfish question — we're no good to anyone if we don't take care of our own needs from time to time. So please don't forget yourself in all of this. You are your own most important customer. When flight attendants give their airline safety pitch before the plane takes off, they instruct you to put on your own oxygen mask first and then help children with theirs. There's a very good reason for this: If you can't take care of yourself, you won't be able to take care of anyone else.

One student's Circle of Customers looked like this:

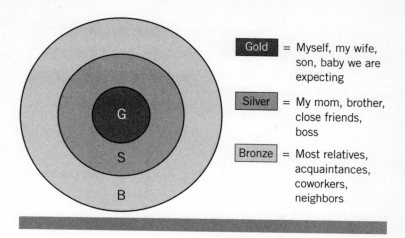

An executive friend of mine travels extensively for his job. One day while on business in California from New York, he called his teenage daughter to check in. When he asked, "How's everything?" she could barely respond. Something had upset her tremendously. Sensing that she was experiencing more than just the usual teen angst, he immediately dropped everything and got on the next plane back East to be with her. She was part of his Gold circle, and his work colleagues, though important to him, were only Silver. That's the sort of customer service you should strive to give your Gold circle members all the time.

If your list is unwieldy, review it again and evaluate it for "quantity versus quality" factors.

Quantity versus Quality

There are people who have many friends and acquaintances (quantity) but whose relationships, for the most part, are shallow and superficial (poor quality). We are social animals and want to interact with, and be liked by, others. It's a very reasonable and important need, as long as we don't get too carried away. It is difficult to manage more than a handful of important relationships. Any manager in business knows that she can only effectively manage a limited number of direct reports — approximately 7 to 10. Any more than that, and she is less effective. This is a sensitive subject and should be handled with great compassion, but consider reducing the number of your customers, or at least creating some distance between you and them. There may be people on your list who sap your energy and spirit. As in business, there are those customers who require tremendous attention but do not seem to contribute much. We all have certain customers who intrude regularly on our lives, who may only be seeking their own self-interests. Developing quality relationships require that we give much of ourselves. Sometimes it's best to part ways; you may have unwittingly set up a codependency that's unhealthy for you and your customer. Reducing your list will free up needed resources enabling you to increase both the quantity and quality of time with your vital few customers.

Once you've completed the Circles of Customers activity, look back at your Priority Pyramid with your key customers in mind. Do any of your priorities change based on what you've discovered here?

To the Horizon and Beyond!

Setting Goals and Uber-Goals

You've done some serious soul-searching up to this point. You've critiqued how you currently live, established a Platinum Standard for how you'd like to live as you go forward, set your broad priorities, and recognized the people who play the most important roles in your life. You know what you want. You're ready to start setting specific goals that will help you get there.

Goal setting plays as crucial a role in your personal life as it does in the business world. Having goals ensures that you are making steady progress toward living the life you want to lead. For example, in order to ensure that he was maintaining a strong marriage — his top priority — my client Bill and his wife Eden set the goal of having one fanciful date per month. Each month, whoever was in charge would tell the other person when the date was scheduled, but would leave the "what" and the "where" a surprise. Instead of doing the usual dinner-and-a-movie thing, Bill and Eden ended up having all sorts of fun adventures. The fact that they'd set a goal of planning fanciful dates encouraged them to maintain their creativity over the course of not just one or two dates, but many.

For each priority you determined in Milestone 3, write down between one and six **Must-Haves** — actions related to the priority that you *must* take in order to live according to your Platinum Standard. For example, for the relationships category, two of your Must-Haves might be to spend more time with your family and keep in better touch with your friends. Your Must-Haves for the emotional well-being category might be to travel more often, to spend more time with your closest friends, or to learn to meditate.

When recording your Must-Haves, don't try to fit in every possible life improvement that you could make. Be selective. Here's a helpful way to think about them. Many years ago, a mentor of mine was giving me advice on how to have a successful career. He said, "Scott, in business, you are always going to have a heap more work on your plate than you can possibly handle. You won't be able to get to everything. In fact, some things will drop by the wayside. But remember, no matter what, *always* do the things that will keep you from getting fired!" He said this in a somewhat tongue-in-cheek manner, but his meaning stuck with me. The message was as relevant to our personal lives as to our jobs: Be sure not to ignore your most important activities and responsibilities.

As you create your Must-Haves, limit them to no more than six per category. As you complete the entire spreadsheet, you may decide to reduce the number to only three per priority. Keep in mind that your Must-Haves should *not* represent a wish list. Rather, they're your "absolutely, positively, must do's" within a given period of time.

I like to do this activity on the computer so I can make a chart that can be changed later, but you can also do this in your notebook if you don't mind recopying and reconfiguring the chart by hand later. Start by putting your priorities in order, as you did in Milestone 3 with the Priority Pyramid. Then write down your Must-Haves for each priority. Here's what a partially completed chart might look like right now:

Priority	Must-Haves
Career achievement	• Earn trust of senior management
	• Be promoted
Physical health	• Reduce blood pressure
	• Lose weight
Emotional well-being	• Learn to meditate

Now that you have a broad idea of what you'd like to accomplish, it's time to get more specific. For each Must-Have, I'd like you to set *short-term* and *long-term goals* that tell you exactly how you're going to achieve it. Short-term goals are ones that you can accomplish within the next week to three months. Long-term goals are ones that will take you four months to a year to accomplish.

All of your goals should be *concrete* and *measurable*,

because only by collecting data on your current performance and comparing it to your future performance will you know for certain that you are making progress. For example, "spending more time with my family" is not a goal; it's a Must-Have. Goals for this Must-Have might be "have dinner with my family at least five nights a week" and "spend every Sunday afternoon with my daughter."

However, before you can determine precise numerical targets such as these, you need to first measure your *baseline performance* for each Must-Have. The baseline measurement tells you how you're doing at achieving this objective right now, so that you can set realistic goals for the future. If your goals are completely out of reach, you will only get discouraged. Measure your current activity level for each of your Must-Haves for at least a week in order to determine your baseline. Then set short- and long-term goals for each one that demand a manageable level of improvement. For example, if you're currently having dinner with your family only one night per week, it's unlikely that you'll immediately be able to change your work schedule in such a way that you'll make it home five nights per week. So set a short-term goal of dinner with your family three nights per week, and a long-term goal of five nights per week.

I'd also like to suggest that you set **uber-goals** for each Must-Have. Uber-goals might take you years to accomplish. They're visionary. Adding them to your chart is going beyond the call of duty. But it's the way you'll eventually become an A-plus player (see Milestone 10) and find yourself leading a truly exceptional life.

Many years ago I set the goal of running at least three times per week. I achieved this goal, but even so I felt dissatisfied that I was averaging no more than two to three miles on each run. So during a momentary lapse of sanity, I decided to set myself the uber-goal of running a marathon.

I knew that I would have to work my way up to this uber-goal gradually. Going from 2 to 26 miles would take significant time and hard work. So, after reading a book about marathon training and speaking to a friend who'd run several races, I gave myself two years to get into shape. I worked backward from there, setting reasonable interim goals. My long-term goal was to run a half-marathon within a year. With that in mind, I put goals in place to increase my mileage per run from 2 to 5 miles within six months, and from 5 to 10 miles within one year. The next year, I slowly increased mileage from there. In the end, I successfully completed a marathon, and I have run several more since.

If you're having difficulty determining what short-term, long-term, and uber-goals to set because you simply have no idea what is realistic for you to achieve within a certain time frame, consider benchmarking. Benchmarking became very popular in corporate America in the late 1980s. Simply put, it means comparing your organization's business practices with your competitor's best-in-class practices. For instance, a company experiencing a

high number of errors and long delays in the billing process might study the billing process of an exemplary company in their own or a related domain to understand how
to improve.

Similarly, when we set brand-new goals for ourselves, it
can be helpful to compare our current and future desired
performance with that of someone who has already accomplished similar goals. Let's say, for example, that you
wanted to completely change direction in your career. To
benchmark, you would identify several people you know
directly or indirectly who have successfully managed a
similar career transition. Ideally, you would then schedule
a face-to-face interview with as many of them as possible
to learn exactly how they approached the situation.

Benchmarking can be applied to any Must-Have.
There's *always* someone else who has blazed a trail before us. We can learn from their successes and failures,
avoiding mistakes they made and picking up tips so that
we can reach our goals more quickly.

Here are some benchmarking pointers:

1. *Benchmark with successful role models.* You should
   have some evidence of people's success, even if that evidence is circumstantial. For instance, if you desire an
   enduring, loving intimate relationship, identify couples
   that have such relationships. You can get an indication
   of this by finding out how many years they've been together, observing how they interact with one another,
   and asking how they've handled tough times.

I think of my Uncle Tony, who married Aunt Mary at age 16. They celebrated 70 years of marriage a few years before he died at age 87. What struck me most about their relationship was how they always interacted with mutual respect and admiration. Even well into their 80s they would hold hands and peck each other on the cheek. This couple had experienced tremendous hardship over the years. They lost their 13-year-old daughter Bunny to cystic fibrosis. Many relationships don't survive this kind of loss. But somehow their experience seemed to give them a greater appreciation for life and the value of relationships. To be sure, I saw them argue, but I also saw how they handled their disagreements. They would never attack the other person in a mean way and never held a grudge. In my mind, they were people I could learn from — benchmark-worthy models.

2. *Choose realistic benchmarking subjects.* When preparing to run my first marathon, I set up a meeting with someone I knew had run his first marathon the year before. I felt that his experience would still be fresh in his mind. I also chose someone whose weight, build, and athleticism were similar to mine. I didn't want to compare myself with someone who had been an Olympic swimmer before running a marathon, for example, because I would only end up setting unrealistic goals for myself.

3. *Be prepared.* Before you meet with people for benchmarking interviews, make sure you have done some

homework. You should know exactly what you want to learn from them. List your objectives as well as your questions. Let the benchmarking subjects know why you want to meet with them and why it's important to you.

4. *Ask lots of questions.* Your questions should foster dialogue. You can best achieve this by beginning your conversation with open-ended questions, which are questions that can't be answered with a simple "yes" or "no." For example, instead of asking, "Did you set goals when you prepared for your first marathon?" ask, "What did you do to prepare for your first marathon?" Once you get the conversation going, ask more specific questions targeting the precise information you need to come up with your goals.

   For instance, in preparing to run a marathon, I asked my benchmarking subjects key questions relating to each significant step in the process: "Explain your training regimen." "What were your milestones along the way?" "How did you handle injuries?" "What kind of food and drink did you have the night before a long training run?" "How did you prepare yourself mentally and physically the night before the marathon?"

5. *Remember to thank the people you interviewed and keep them updated on your progress.* The people who helped you will be interested in knowing that they had a hand in your success. They may also provide useful guidance for the unexpected problems, issues, and challenges that are sure to arise along the way.

And if you're really having trouble coming up with any goals at all, try this activity.

ACTIVITY: Idea Juicing

Have you ever used a citrus juicer to squeeze every last drop of fresh, delicious juice out of an orange? Wouldn't it be great if you had a similar tool for squeezing ideas out of your brain? Well, I do, and I call it Idea Juicing. It's a creative process for identifying possible Must-Haves, goals, and uber-goals if you're at a loss for ideas.

Look at your list of priorities. Pick just one category to begin. Now write down every single idea that comes to mind for how you could improve your life in this category, whether you think it's stupid or silly or unrealistic or not. You'll go back later to filter through and select the ideas that you think will make the best Must-Haves and short-term, long-term, and uber-goals. I find it best to engage in this process with at least one other person. Hearing their ideas is one way to get your creative juices flowing.

For instance, one of my goals is to spend Sunday afternoons with my family. But we don't always know what we want to do with this time together. And so we use Idea Juicing to come up with unusual, exciting activities. We'll list every possibility, from going to the park for a picnic, to staying in and playing games, regardless of how far-fetched it might seem (are we really going to fly to Florida to go to Disney World today? I don't think so). Then we narrow down our possibilities later and come up with a solution that makes everyone in the family happy.

The most important rules for Idea Juicing are as follows:

- Don't criticize or evaluate ideas as you go. It's easy to dismiss some suggestions, such as the goal of writing a book or learning to play a musical instrument, as unattainable. But perhaps you'll decide to make these uber-goals. Why not plan a trip to Disney World for next summer's vacation?
- Generate as many ideas as possible. Then take a break and brainstorm more.
- Have fun. Challenge each other to be crazy, silly, and absurd. And don't forget to laugh!

Goal setting will continue to play a crucial role as you move forward and implement your Exceptional Living Plan. As Jesse Stoner and Drea Zigarmi put it in their management guide, *From Vision to Reality:* "The best way to predict your future is to create it."

Now You've Got It

Putting It All Together

If you had a boss in your personal life, and you walked into his office and told him about all these great priorities, goals, and uber-goals that you'd come up with to improve yourself, I bet he'd be impressed. But he'd also say, "Listen, you've got lots of terrific ideas here. Now you need to put it all together."

With the first five milestones, you've determined how you want to be living your life and you've set broad as well as specific goals to help you get there. The next step is to put all of those ideas into a concrete action plan, the map that will enable you to get from where you are to where you'd like to be: You're going to create your **Exceptional Living Plan.**

The Exceptional Living Plan is the ultimate tool for organizing all the work you've done so far. It *is* your plan of action, your life map. It's a record of all the priorities and goals you've set for yourself, of where you've been and where you're trying to go. This could be the most valuable work you've done in this process, so please take it seriously.

Creating an Exceptional Living Plan enables you to see the trade-offs and payoffs involved in the decisions that you make. It provides context so that you can view your entire life as an interconnected web. Let's say, for example, that you're considering going to graduate school. Adding grad school as a Must-Have under the career achievement category and filling in the respective columns would illustrate the fact that some of your other priorities will have to change in order for you to accomplish this goal. You may not be able to make it to the gym five times a week or spend every weekend with your family. Consider your Gold Circle customers. Given the impact grad school will have on you and them, is it worthwhile?

Kim attended a personal effectiveness seminar that I led about 10 years ago. When she met me, her husband had just left her with their two young kids to raise alone, without a job. She was convinced that she was going to lose the house, custody of her children — everything. She was totally panicked. But during the course of the hours we spent together, I coached her on some specific actions she could take to get through her challenges. I helped her create her Exceptional Living Plan, outlining precisely how to move forward, and worked to build the confidence she required to see it through. On that day, she made a promise to herself to be the best role model to her children that she could be. She vowed to take a real estate course. Just a short while later, she finished the course and started working again. She did well and was able to make the payments on the house by herself. Both of her kids are in college now, and she owns her home. She still writes every so often to thank me for helping her get her life back together.

Here's what Kim told me once about her Exceptional Living Plan: "I've really stuck with it since taking the class. It helps me stay focused on achieving my goals. But even more importantly, it reminds me of who I want to be, where my values and priorities lie. I refer to and update my chart all the time. And I've encouraged most of my friends and even my kids to make a plan for themselves, too!"

ACTIVITY: The Exceptional Living Plan

Here's how it works:

1. Go back to the chart listing your priorities and Must-Haves, which you began to create with Milestone 5. Your priorities should be in the leftmost column, listed in order of their importance. Your Must-Haves for each priority should be recorded in the very next column.

2. Write your Platinum Standard from Milestone 2 at the top of your plan. This will remind you that all decisions you make and goals you set should be in the context of living your life according to your vision.

3. Insert a column between the priority and Must-Haves columns, and name it "Customers." In this column, list which Circles of Customers, from Milestone 4, each priority most impacts.

4. Add four more columns to the right of the Must-Haves column. In these, list your baseline measurements and short-term, long-term, and uber-goals from Milestone 5.

You should not expect to fill out every box in your Exceptional Living Plan right away. You might still be in the process of collecting data to determine your baseline measurements and, based on those, setting goals for some of your Must-Haves over the next few weeks. Just take a first stab at putting the plans you've generated so far into a usable format that you can track easily.

Once you've completed a draft, print your chart out or make a copy of it and put it up on your office wall or refrigerator door, someplace where you'll see it frequently. Let it serve as a constant visual reminder of the exceptional life you are aiming to achieve.

At the same time, keep in mind that this should be a *living* document. The advantage of creating it on your computer is that you'll be able to easily edit it down the road. Don't feel that you must stick to your first version. Revise away. After all, your goals and aspirations, like you, are constantly changing. (Only your Platinum Standard isn't.)

The following table is an example of what an Exceptional Living Plan might look like when you're finished.

Congratulations! You've got an Exceptional Life Plan that will help you move from the Complacent or Crisis Zone to the Purpose Zone.

Platinum Standard: To be the best I can be every day, and in doing so, to make richer the lives of those around me.

Priority	Customers	Must-Haves	Baseline	Short-Term Goals	Long-Term Goals	Uber-Goals
Relationships	*Gold:* myself, my wife, my son	Spend more quality time with family	75% of time on weekends, 2-3 hours per day on weekdays	Breakfast together every day. Get home earlier 2 times per week	Work from home minimum of 1 day per week	New job that encourages shorter hours/more work from home
	Bronze: friends	Be in touch with friends more often	Meet 1-4 times per month. E-mail/phone sometimes	Increase frequency of contact by 10%	Find regular events/do sports to meet up	Graduate from school
Career	*Gold:* myself *Silver:* my boss	Find new job with flexibility at growth company	Small company with no growth, no flexibility	Start researching/ send resumes	Find new job within 3 months of graduation	Meet new people to network with
Physical	*Gold:* myself	Eat better	Lunch out every day	Bag lunch 2 times per week	Bag lunch 3 times per week	Cook more healthy dinners
		Exercise more	Go to gym 2 times per week	Go to gym 4 times per week	Go to gym 5 times per week	

(continued)

Platinum Standard (continued)

Priority	Customers	Must-Haves	Baseline	Short-Term Goals	Long-Term Goals	Uber-Goals
Financial	Gold: myself, my family	Eliminate debt, save money	$20k debt from school loan	Pay off student loan	Save $200 per week	Save enough for down payment for home purchase
Intellectual	Gold: myself	Learn to play guitar	Can't play at all	Buy guitar. Find teacher	Lessons 2 times per month	Be able to play for family
Spiritual	Gold: myself Bronze: my community	Attend church regularly	Only attend at Christmas and Easter	Attend 1 time per month	Attend every week	Take leadership role
Emotional	Gold: myself	Take time for myself	Minimal time for fun	(See guitar, friends)	(See guitar, friends)	Get outdoors during lunch time

Interlude

Phase III

Turning Your Plan into Reality

Over the next nine weeks, you will begin the implementation phase of your Exceptional Living Plan. This is perhaps the most critical stage in reaching your life goals, because without implementation even the best-laid plans will not be accomplished. And yet, in the business world and in our personal lives, it's a step that often gets left behind as an afterthought.

I mentioned earlier that I have a producer friend who wants to be in front of the camera rather than behind it. She definitely knows what she wants and where her priorities lie. She even knows how to get there . . . at least in theory. The problem is, she hasn't done anything to make her dream come true. She falls short when it comes to implementation. (I hope she reads this book!)

I urge you: Please don't let your Exceptional Living Plan become a wall decoration. Follow through with it. Turn your vision into reality.

Now that you have a plan, consider how you are liv-

ing your life right now. It's time to begin making changes. You need to start the process of navigating your way out of the Crisis and Complacency Zones and into the Purpose Zone. Accomplishing these four milestones will take you through that process.

First, in Milestone 7, you'll zero in on which areas of your life most need fixing — the places where you're going to have the most trouble reaching your goals because your baseline is so far from your ideal. With Milestone 8, you'll put out the fires that have been keeping you trapped in the Crisis Zone. With Milestone 9, you'll exit the Complacency Zone by learning to wow your customers rather than taking them for granted. You'll enable yourself to enter the Purpose Zone with Milestone 10 by practicing empowerment. And you'll fully realize your new status as an A-plus player by reaching for your highest goals with Milestone 11.

A Picture Is Worth a Thousand Words

Figuring Out What's Working and What's Not

At the age of 28, Jack is already 30 pounds overweight and gaining fast. He and his wife want to have kids. But with a history of obesity and diabetes in his family, Jack knows that if he doesn't take control of his weight right away, it could end up posing a serious threat to his health in the future.

When I started working with Jack a year ago, he told me of his weight loss goals, but also complained that he'd tried every diet out there with no success. I explained that most weight loss books lack in two areas: (1) They don't tie your weight loss to a larger life goal, and (2) they don't get you to follow through on your plan. I then emphasized the critical nature of tracking his progress in numbers. I told Jack, "Well-run businesses know that what gets measured gets done." I worked with him to make a plan for exercising and eating right with achievable and measurable goals. He keeps track of his progress on a spreadsheet, and even found that he enjoyed creating graphs and charts with the aid of a simple computer program. In addition, I told him to think of his weight loss plan in the context of his overall life goals — being able to play with his kids and see them grow up. Then I had him commit to his plan publicly by sending an e-mail out to his closest friends and family members.

It worked. In just six weeks, Jack lost 10 pounds. And that was over the holiday season, when most people gain weight. He also reports that his relationship with his wife has improved because she had begun to resent his weight gain, viewing him as not committed to good health and vital living habits. He then created and implemented a plan for losing the next 20 pounds, which took him just a few months more. Jack continues to want to see his body change for the better, so he has now begun to formulate increased goals for weight training at the gym. I have no doubt that he'll succeed.

You know your goals, you understand how they connect to your Platinum Standard, and you even have a sense of which priorities need to shift. But in order to execute your Exceptional Living Plan, you need more information. It's time to take a close look at the landscape of your life. You've got to get down to the nitty-gritty level of collecting and analyzing data so that you can figure out what's working and what's not. Data collection will help you identify where the biggest gaps lie between how you're actually living and how you want to be living. You should begin this step immediately, while you start working to achieve two to three of your short-term goals. Let's hit the ground running!

Data is an extremely useful tool for businesses and for individuals. It gets goals that you're trying to pursue and problems that you're trying to solve out of the theoretical range and into the realm of hardcore reality. It removes subjectivity and conjecture. My former consulting colleagues and I had a saying: "In God we trust; all others bring data." Furthermore, you can't improve what you can't measure. You have to know where you're starting from, where you're going, and how you're doing along the way.

Most of us are off target when we rely on memory or perceptions. To prove my point, think of how many hours you spend watching television each week and write down the number. Then for the next week, assuming normal circumstances, record your actual time spent watching television. Be honest with yourself. Don't decrease your normal viewing hours during this period. Now compare your perception with reality. If television isn't your thing, substitute something else (time spent surfing the Internet, talking on the phone, etc.). I bet you anything you underestimated.

My wife, Catherine, and I used to have frequent disagreements over who was responsible for the fact that we weren't meeting our monthly savings targets — until we started collecting data. For one month, we each carefully tracked every penny that we spent. In the end, we realized that *both* of us were responsible for the shortfall. She'd buy an extra item of clothing for our daughter Jennifer; I'd go out to lunch rather than eating my brown-bag meal. We agreed to make changes in another expense category rather than give up these small personal luxuries, and soon we were meeting our savings targets.

Go back to your Exceptional Living Plan. Do you feel that you know what you need to do to accomplish your Must-Haves? Are there any gaps in the chart where you haven't yet measured your baseline performance, or set short- or long-term goals? Don't try to collect data for every single Must-Have, since you'll merely overwhelm yourself. Instead, focus your data-gathering efforts wherever you feel that you don't have a handle on the problems that you're trying to overcome or need more information in order to accomplish your goals.

You can't cut corners with data collection. Only good, conclusive data will help you reach your goals. So take a full four weeks for this step — if you want to figure out what's going wrong, you'll need data that truly represents your life the way you're currently living it.

ACTIVITY: Picturization

You can't just gather data; you have to analyze it, or it won't be of any use to you. And the easiest way to conduct an analysis is to translate the data into visual form with a chart or a graph. I call this **Picturization.**

Here's how Picturization works:

1. *Identify your information needs.* Do you have a solid understanding of where you are now and where you're trying to go with your priorities, especially the top three? What is your baseline measurement for each Must-Have within these three categories? Where do you need to gather more information in order to create effective, practical goals? Efficient data collection begins with asking these questions.

   For instance, like many people today, you may be attempting to achieve a better "work-life balance." But in order to create specific goals toward getting there, you have to figure out where and how your time is currently being spent. Your information needs may include the following:

   - "How many hours am I spending at work each week?"
   - "How am I spending my working hours by category?" (e.g., internal meetings, traveling, customer visits, e-mail, etc.)
   - "How am I spending my nonworking hours by category?"

2. *Prepare your data collection method.* The simplest method for data collection is a data sheet. This is a chart providing space for recording a specific value or action.

   For example, here is the checklist created by Dr. Harry Roberts, a professor at the University of Chicago business school who wanted to find out exactly where he was being unproductive in his life so that he could better manage his problems:

Week of_____

Improvement Opportunity	Mon	Tues	Wed	Thurs	Fri	Sat	Sun	Total
Was late for an appointment or meeting	II	I		I	II			6
Searched for something misplaced or lost	I		I				I	3
Delayed return of phone call or reply to email	III	IIII	II	II	III	I	II	17
Put a small task in a hold pile	I	I			I			3
Failed to discard incoming junk mail promptly		I	I			II		4

3. *Collect the data.* Here are a few tips for data collection:

 - Data should be quantitative rather than qualitative (e.g., "number of hours worked: 12" rather than "worked too late").
 - Collect data in real time as often as possible. Memory is unreliable.
 - Be honest. After all, you're doing this for your own self-improvement.
 - Gather enough data to ensure that it is representative. For example, if you want to know how often you lose your temper, track the number of times you do so every day for a week. If you want to know

how many hours a week you're working on average, don't pick the week before a major deadline to track the information.

4. *Picturize the data.* Your data won't do you much good if you're just looking at a bunch of random numbers. You need to view it in the form of a bar chart or graph. You can make charts out of just about any data: how many hours of sleep you're getting, the number of nights you have dinner with your family, your debt, and so on. This is very easy to do with Excel, but you can also do it manually with graph paper.

Let's say that you're trying to lower your weight as a Must-Have for your healthy living priority, but you're not exactly sure what kind of goals you should set for getting there. You could measure your weight and record the number every day for a month. At the end of the month, you'd be able to tell if the ending number was higher or lower than the starting number, but not much else. If you put the data into a line graph, however, you'd be able to see the particular

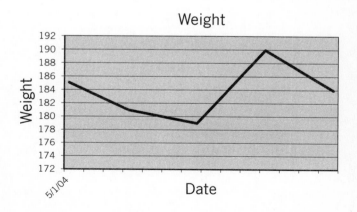

days when your weight rose or fell. You'd also be able to detect an overall trend toward improvement or not.

5. *Use the picture to determine your next steps.* Now that you have a chart showing that your weight spiked on a particular day, focus in further and try to determine why it spiked. On days when your weight rose above a certain level, did you have a stressful day? Eat an especially heavy meal? Forget to stick to your exercise regimen? You can see how conducting this analysis will help you deal with your problem.

Gathering and putting together data in this way gives you insight into why you're living in the Crisis or Complacency Zone. It tells you where you need to focus your efforts so that you can solve your problems and move into the Purpose Zone. Now let's begin the process of finding and implementing solutions.

Firefighting

Leaving the Crisis Zone

Some time ago, a friend came to me seeking advice. He was definitely in the Crisis Zone. He told me that he was suffering from all kinds of problems: He didn't have enough money to pay his bills, his career seemed stalled, and his relationship with his girlfriend was rocky. After hearing him out, I tried to help steer him through some of his issues.

At the end of our conversation, he made a comment that stuck with me to this day: "Gee Scott, you sure are lucky."

"Why is that?" I replied.

"Well, you never seem to have any problems."

All I could think at the time was "If you only knew!" As I reflected on the comment later, I thought, "I really have no more (or fewer) problems than the average person." It's just that some people like my friend walk around with what I call a problem mentality. They develop the attitude that they are victims in life. So rather than focusing on taking a positive approach to managing and dealing with their issues, they go through life wondering why they've been dealt such a lousy hand.

One of the first steps you must take in order to leave the Crisis Zone is to reconcile yourself to the fact that *problems are a fact of life!* No one — no matter how rich, successful, or good-looking — is immune from day-to-day ups and downs. In fact, I would go so far as to say that in terms of human development, problems are actually a good thing. Why? Because they offer opportunities for growth. We may not always ask for such "opportunities" to arise, but I assure you that we always have something to learn from them. Confronting problems makes us wiser. As Nietzsche said, "That which does not kill me, makes me stronger." We are much better off putting the time and energy we usually spend trying to run away from our problems or cover them up into dealing directly with them, tackling them head on.

Each year for the past 10 years, I have asked my Fordham University students, "How do you solve problems?" Their typical response: "First, I freak out and panic. Then when I calm down, I apply a band-aid solution to get quickly past it."

Think about how you address issues in your life. Are you generally effective? Do you have a logical, disciplined approach, or is it more haphazard? Do you frequently find yourself shooting from the hip? Perhaps it's time to change your approach. This chapter will give you some ideas for how to go about just that.

In implementing your Exceptional Living Plan, you need to put out any fires that are burning before you can focus on fixing smaller problems and making progress toward your grander life vision. Look at it this way: An alcoholic is living in the Crisis Zone. She first and foremost needs to stop drinking in order to exit the Crisis Zone. Only once she's done that can she start working toward her long-term goal of founding a company — a goal that will take her out of the Complacency Zone and into the Purpose Zone.

A new client, Joe, serves as an example of someone who let a fire burn for too long. He called me up one day in a panic. "My wife told me today that she's going to leave me!" he exclaimed in disbelief. "I don't understand it at all. We just had a fancy anniversary dinner last week. This is completely out of the blue!"

The thing is, after some examination, it became obvious that this wasn't "completely out of the blue." Joe is a sports fanatic. He's either out playing golf or watching sporting events on TV year round. When he and his wife were married 15 years ago, Sara accepted his habits with a "That's just the way Joe is!" kind of attitude. But then they had two kids, and Joe's job changed so that he had to be away from home more often. Instead of helping Sara cope with the increased stress, Joe escaped into sports more than ever. Sara became increasingly fed up, but Joe did nothing to change. He was deep in the Complacency Zone, doing only the bare minimum to keep his increasingly average marriage alive. Eventually, Sara couldn't handle it anymore. That's when she announced that she was leaving him. And she did.

If Joe had leapt into action and focused attention on his wife's unhappiness before it overwhelmed her, he might have been able to salvage his marriage. But unfortunately, he did not. Don't let this happen to you.

Take out your Exceptional Living Plan. Collect the data necessary to fill in any missing baseline measurements, and compare these to your Platinum Standard of how you'd like to be living your life. Where do the largest gaps between your ideal life and reality lie? These are the areas where you've got fires burning, and so you should devote your immediate attention to putting out the fires. Focus on why these are problem areas for you, and start to figure out solutions.

But first you need to determine whether what you're experiencing is actually a problem. You've heard the old saying "A well-defined problem is a problem half solved." I have found this to hold true. What it means to me is that some people are unable to distinguish between a problem and a fact of life. My friend and mentor Fred Smith, a very successful retired Dallas businessman, puts it this way: "A problem is something we can do something about; a fact of life is not." He then holds up his right hand, withered since birth, and says, "This old withered hand of mine is not my problem, it is my fact!" All the stressing out, fuming, and fretting in the world will not make Fred's hand whole again. So his attitude is, don't spend any time worrying about it! The next time you're facing what seems to be an insurmountable problem, ask yourself, "Is this a problem or is it my fact?" If it's something you can do something about, then you have a call to action. Start planning how you're going to tackle it. If not, endeavor to gracefully accept it as fact, and be at peace with it.

Once you have defined the problems that you want to work on, do some brainstorming to generate a broad list of options for how to go about solving them. It's good practice to start with a long list and then narrow it down to the one to two remedies that you feel will have the maximum impact. Be aware that your initial options list will probably be overwhelming and complex. You may not know where to start. Our problems don't usually come to us wrapped up in neat little packages. Rather, they're more often an entanglement of issues, emotions, misunderstandings, and misperceptions. In fact, the precise nature of a problem is often unclear because we're not very good at articulating it. We have to straighten out our language. We often describe problems by identifying their *symptoms* ("my head hurts"), or *causes* ("I bumped my head"), or *solutions* ("I need an aspirin"). But the actual *problem* in this example is that "as a *result* of having a headache, I am unable to finish my report by tomorrow's deadline."

The following definitions may prove helpful to you in defining and brainstorming solutions to your problems:

Symptom = Evidence of a problem
Problem = A negative factor that directly affects
                performance

Cause   = What created the problem
Solution = Action that removes the cause of the
                  problem

The following table gives a few examples.

Symptom	Problem	Cause	Solution
Rushing too much	Lateness for important meetings	Poor time management	Prioritize and plan
Losing temper	Strained interpersonal relationships	• Lack of sleep • Pressure/stress • Overwork	• Make sleep a priority • Learn relaxation techniques • Reduce workload
Misplacing things	Spending too much time looking for things	• Forgetfulness • Absentmindedness	Develop foolproof system and stick with it

As you review your brainstormed list, see if you can tease out your actual problems, because that's where you'll find your solutions.

Now you need to pick and choose from your list of possible solutions, determining which one (or ones) you want to implement. The secret to making good decisions is being objective in what is normally a subjective and emotional process. Evaluating each solution according to the following criteria will help you evaluate your choices so that you can decide which will be the most effective.

1. Impact on problem
   To what degree will the remedy relieve me of my problem?
2. Impact on priorities
   Referring to my Life Plan, how many priorities will be favorably impacted by the remedy?
3. Impact on customers
   Which remedy will most delight my Gold Circle customers?
4. Cost-benefit analysis
   Which remedy will yield the highest return on investment?
5. Ease of implementation
   Which remedy will have the least overall resistance or the fewest negative consequences associated with it?
6. Quality of life
   Which remedy contributes most to the overall quality of my life?
7. Consistency with guiding principles
   Which remedy is most consistent with my Platinum Standard?

After careful analysis and consideration, you may conclude that the cure is worse than the disease. In other words, you may feel that none of your potential remedies make sense at this time. That's okay. Sometimes not doing anything is a reasonable choice. At least you've made an informed decision. However, I'd like to suggest that whenever possible you enlist the help of a close friend or mentor to help you think through the decision-making process, because often other people can find solutions to our problems that we simply can't see ourselves when we're in the thick of things.

Now you're ready for the implementation phase. Acting on a decision is usually more difficult than making it. We know what we have to do, but we fail to take action. We drag our feet, stalling, hoping that the problem will just disappear without our having to do anything about it at all. If only life were that simple! Sometimes we fail to take action because we lack the courage or resolve. We become weak-kneed and wishy-washy. It is during these times that we need to revisit our Platinum Standards, re-establishing our sense of urgency and conviction. You've come this far; now follow through!

In order to ensure that you implement the solutions you've come up with, translate them into short- and long-term goals: short-term goals for smaller issues such as getting to work on time, long-term goals for larger issues such as losing weight.

By now you've probably noticed that problem solving can be an involved process. Please note: I do not suggest applying this methodology to every little difficulty that comes along. It would be too unmanageable. Use it only for solving the issues that are most impacting your ability to obtain your overall objectives.

Several years ago, I presented what proved to be a great concept at a company that was experiencing major quality problems. The president was eager to have all the employees involved. So I introduced an initiative that I called "100 Improvements in 100 Days." The idea was to have each of the company's 100 employees identify and implement one quality improvement project within a 100-day period. The results were fantastic! The employees found ways to enhance customer satisfaction, improve safety, increase efficiency, and remove petty annoyances.

You can make use of the "100/100" initiative in your personal life, as well, though you may want to set a more modest target, such as three improvements in three weeks. Modify the program to suit your own situation. If you have children, get them involved in thinking of ways to improve quality of life at home for the entire family. Be sure that all of the ideas they generate are specific and can be implemented with minimal investment.

The good news is that solving even seemingly big problems — ones that may be keeping you in the Crisis Zone — isn't as difficult as you might think if you apply a methodology. For example, for the critical problem of losing your temper, your short-term goal might be to practice breathing exercises for 15 minutes in the car every night when you get home from work before you walk into the house. Your long-term goal might be to do weekly psychotherapy to learn better anger management tactics. Enter these goals into your Exceptional Living Plan. You should be filling in most of the gaps by now.

When you come up against a brick wall, don't panic. Solicit the assistance of someone who has emotional distance from the problem. That's what companies do when they're in trouble, after all: They call in consultants! En-list a friend, family member, or trusted figure such as a therapist or religious leader to help you figure things out and come up with a plan of action if yours isn't working. I bet they'll have solid advice.

Or try the Five Why's to get at the root cause of the problem.

ACTIVITY: The Five Why's

When my clients are confronting issues that they can't find solutions for, I often find it's because they're not de-fining their problems properly. Usually, the managers are chasing down the symptoms rather than trying to discover and do something about the root cause. They're plugging up the leaky holes instead of turning off the faucet, so to speak.

There are a number of techniques that we use in busi-ness to determine the root cause of a problem. But I find one of the simplest and most effective to be the Five Why's. All it involves is asking "why" five times and giving yourself five answers.

Here's an example of how it works in the business world: Researchers at the National Park Service in Wash-ington, D.C., were struggling to figure out why the Jeffer-son Memorial was deteriorating so rapidly. And so they called in a team of experts to help them ask and answer the Five Why's:

1. Why is the Jefferson Memorial deteriorating? → Because it is scrubbed clean so often.
2. Why does it need to be scrubbed so often? → Because
   it's covered in sparrow droppings.
3. Why is it covered in sparrow droppings? → Because
   the sparrows are feeding on the masses of spiders gathered in the building.
4. Why are there so many spiders in the building? → Because the spiders like to eat small insects called midges,
   which gather in the building in large numbers.
5. Why are there so many midges in the building? → Because they're attracted to the floodlights (used to light
   up the Memorial at night), which come on each day
   at sunset, the exact time when midges come out en
   masse to mate.

After speaking with entomologists, the Park Service
determined a very straightforward solution to the problem: Turn the floodlights on one hour later, after the
midges' mating time was over. This simple act substantially reduced the number of midges in the building,
which unraveled the entire chain of events leading to the
need for frequent washings in the first place.

It's easy to see how you can apply the Five Why's to
your personal life in order to come up with the root cause
of a problem. From there, you can determine the specific
steps you need to take to improve the situation.

Let's say, for example, that you're chronically late for
work. Ask the Five Why's:

1. Why am I late for work? → Because I don't leave the
   house early enough.

2. Why don't I leave the house early enough? → Because I don't have adequate time to shower, dress, and eat breakfast.
3. Why don't I have time for my morning routine? → Because I don't get up early enough.
4. Why don't I get up early enough? → Because I hit the snooze button five times.
5. Why do I hit the snooze button? → Because I'm so tired in the morning.

Root cause = Too tired in the morning. Solution = Go to bed earlier at night.

You could then do the Five Why's again to determine why you don't go to bed earlier.

As long as you're honest with yourself, you should be able to find the root causes of most problems. Knock down these barriers one by one by setting goals that will help keep you on track to implementing solutions, and you'll find yourself moving closer than ever to living the exceptional life you've been dreaming of living.

The Art of Anticipation

Wowing Your Customers

Achieving a truly exceptional life requires taking care of yourself *and* others. You've taken the first critical step in getting yourself out of the Crisis Zone. You've figured out what you want out of life and begun stamping out any active fires that were burning. With these milestones in place, you're already moving closer to living according to your Platinum Standard.

Now you can take a bit of the focus off yourself and shift it onto others. After all, without friends and family, how fulfilling can your life really be? It's time to stop taking your loved ones for granted and start treating them like the valued customers they are.

In Phase Two, you identified and organized your list of customers in order of priority. You put them into your Exceptional Living Plan. Now, in Phase Three, the implementation phase, the real work begins. You need to develop a customer service mentality that will enable you to meet your own goals while satisfying the needs of the most important people in your life.

How are you going to discover your customers' needs so that you can find ways to meet and even exceed their expectations? The obvious answer is "Just ask them." But good communication can prove tricky. In fact, I find it's one of the most difficult — but also most crucial — skills required for success in business and life in general.

Here are some tips for better communication:

- Schedule important conversations in advance. Don't try to bring up touchy subjects over breakfast as you're rushing off to work. Serious talks require dedicated time.
- Once you've set a meeting, plan what you're going to say. You may even want to write down a few notes.
- When you're ready to meet, prepare an optimal environment free from distractions. If you're having a discussion with your partner, be sure the kids have already gone to bed. If the talk is with a difficult coworker, have it outside the office.
- During the talk, be precise in your word choice. Try not to make broad accusations, but bring up specific examples whenever possible.
- Connect with the person you're speaking with through eye contact and open body language. Give nonverbal cues such as nods and "uh-huh."
- Listen carefully to what the other person is saying and paraphrase it. Encourage her or him to be specific.

If your husband says, "You don't pay attention to me anymore," ask him what exactly he means. You're not spending enough time together? You're not asking enough questions about his day? You seem distracted when you do talk?

- At the end of the conversation, establish the next steps. If you've had a disagreement, brainstorm solutions. What can each of you do to improve the situation?

Even if you make an outstanding effort to discuss your customers' needs with them, a conversation may not always suffice. Sometimes people just don't know what they want or are unable to articulate their needs clearly. Sometimes they're too shy to say it. But almost everyone appreciates it when you notice things without even asking and *anticipate* their needs.

Delivering exceptional customer service requires you to act like an anthropologist. You can learn a lot about your customers by observing their habits and behaviors. Imagine, for example, that you need to pick out a birthday present for your mother-in-law. The worst sort of customer service would be to forget her birthday completely. The next best level of customer service would be to call and ask her what she wants, then buy that gift for her. She'd most likely be satisfied, but not overly delighted. The optimal level of customer service would be to pay attention to what she says and does, and figure out on your own what she might like to receive. This is the sort of customer service that pleasantly surprises people and makes them truly happy in their relationships. Why not be an *exceptional* son-in-law rather than an average one?

Check in with your customers frequently by asking them questions and simply observing their behavior. Who knows what you might discover?

ACTIVITY: Quick Pulse Check

We lead hectic lives. We're usually operating in overdrive. And so it's easy to make excuses not to communicate with our key customers.

Developing a customized Quick Pulse Check can provide you with a fun and efficient way to survey the people you care about. It will tell you at a glance how you're doing at meeting their needs and provide early warning signs of potential problems. What's more, it will give you ideas for how you can delight your customers.

Here are examples of some questions that you might include on your Quick Pulse Check. Feel free to adapt it as you wish, depending on the person and the situation. For example, if you and your spouse are arguing about finances, you might want to include specific questions concerning that topic.

Please rate the following questions on a scale from 1 to 5 (1= not at all, 3 = neutral, 5 = very much):

1. Have I been meeting your expectations? _____
2. Have I been exceeding your expectations? _____
3. Do you feel that we have been getting along well? _____

4. Do you feel that we have been talking often enough? _____

5. Do you feel that we have been spending enough quality time together? _____

6. Do you feel that I'm aware of what's going on in your life? _____

7. Do you feel that you're aware of what's going on in my life? _____

Now please provide short answers to these questions:

8. Have I done anything in the past month that particularly upset you? _____
If so, please describe: _____

9. Have I done anything in the past month that particularly pleased you? _____
If so, please describe: _____

10. Do you have any specific recommendations for how to improve our relationship? _____

Hand the survey out to your Gold Circle customers at least once a month (in paper form or by e-mail). Start today. Then follow up on any answers that surprised you. Don't do it right away, but rather schedule a meeting for later. That way, you can ask your customers for more specific feedback about how to deliver exceptional service to them in the future.

Building rapport with your customers will help ensure caring, enduring relationships. This is a crucial step in moving out of the Complacency Zone, a zone in which you accept life as it is, and into the Purpose Zone, a zone in which you actively try to make life better for yourself and those around you. Developing an outstanding customer service ethic in your personal life will not only make the people you're closest to happier, it will also help you realize the goals you set forth in your Exceptional Living Plan. Just as an intelligent CEO relies on his employees to make the company successful, so must you rely on and simultaneously look out for the best interests of others to make your dreams reality. If you treat your customers well, they will help you attain your goals. If you treat them poorly, they can prove the biggest obstacles to success.

At the end of *The Wizard of Oz*, the Wizard tells the Tin Man, who is in search of a heart: "Remember, my friend: A man's heart is judged not by how much he loves, but by how much he is loved by others." That is the true meaning of customer service — putting your heart into the service you provide.

Milestone 10, Weeks 12–13

Free to Be

Empowering Yourself and Others

You've successfully made your way out of the Crisis and Complacency Zones. You've taken care of your own major problems, and you've focused attention on meeting and even exceeding the needs of the people who matter most to you. Now you're ready to take yourself to the next level — to start working your way into the Purpose Zone.

In order to succeed, we must remove obstacles that tend to undermine our belief in ourselves and others, thereby stunting our growth and limiting our creativity. The kind of obstacle that I am referring to is disempowerment. Disempowerment is an oppressive state that is either self-induced — usually the result of conditioning in the early formative years of our development — or caused by others. If you feel that others are responsible for holding you back from reaching your goals, then I hope you can change your life circumstances. Perhaps you need to go back to earlier chapters in the book and get out of a

Crisis Zone before you can move into the Purpose Zone. But I also want to ask you to be honest with yourself. In many cases, we are responsible for our own disempowerment. We keep ourselves from moving forward. This chapter will discuss what true empowerment is and offer tools to help you become more empowered.

You will receive a dual benefit in reading this chapter. First, self-empowerment is a prerequisite for entering the Purpose Zone. Empowering yourself means becoming the most self-assured, and therefore effective, person you can be. Second, empowerment is not only about you. It is also about empowering others: spouse, children, employees, and yes, even your boss! When you empower others, you unearth hidden potential like treasure buried deep beneath the surface of the ground. Empowering others means seeing how they can play a role in helping you achieve your life goals, while simultaneously helping them build their own skill sets. Empowering others can be a truly liberating experience. Too often we cling to the responsibility for tasks, activities, and projects without ever allowing others to lend a hand. This hurts us in two ways. First, it prevents us from moving on to more value-added kinds of activities that are also "on strategy." Second, we deny others opportunities by refusing to delegate tasks. By delegating, we help others learn, develop, and grow into their own potential.

To some extent, we are products of our past, and our pasts may have included a degree of negative programming. We come into this world as naturally confident, curious, and courageous individuals. For many of us, though, well-intentioned parents, caregivers, and other significant people in our lives erode or diminish our natural positive state. The disempowering messages begin very early on. The average child hears the word *no* 10 times more often than the word *yes*. As parents we justify this discrepancy by saying we are only trying to protect our children from harm. Although this is largely true, upon closer investigation we discover other reasons. For instance, we may tell our child that he or she can't do something out of convenience for ourselves. It takes too much time, energy, and patience to empower our children. It's easier to just say no. Some parents may simply be passing their own beliefs, biases, and prejudices on to their children. When I asked my mom why she had never continued her education after high school, she told me that her father had told her not to bother — "women don't do that kind of thing; they just get married, have children, and take care of their families."

Negative programming is a result of the messages we receive throughout our lives. Here are some examples: "Why can't you be more like your older brother?" "Please don't touch that, you'll break it for sure." "Don't do that; you'll get hurt." "You're not smart/tall/big/fast enough." "Just face it, you don't have the same opportunities as others." "Accept who you are." In one way or another, and with varying degrees of influence, these messages are examples of how we become conditioned to think, believe, and react throughout life.

This conditioning alters our perceptions in life and in many ways distorts reality — which is that we have the ability to do amazing things. Empowerment requires strong self-esteem, but self-esteem can be easily destroyed for some people. Unfortunately, we perpetuate disempowerment by surrounding ourselves with people — in both our personal and professional lives — who want to play the role of protector. People with low self-esteem often are attracted to stronger, more dominant personalities who will play the role of protector or benevolent dictator. What can we do about the disempowering factors in our lives? With regard to the early childhood experiences, we should simply recognize that we may have experienced a degree of negative programming, but that with some practice, we can deprogram our thinking.

The concept of empowerment comes straight out of the corporate world. It was developed as a tool to provide employees at all levels of an organization with the authority and responsibility for making their own decisions. For example, at some retail stores empowered clerks are allowed to accept returns of under, say, $1,000 in value, rather than always having to call in a supervisor to execute the task. This makes the clerks feel more trusted and important, and it pleases you as a customer, because you don't have to wait as long to get your money back.

On a personal level, empowering yourself means believing in your ability to execute your vision and fulfill your dreams. Think of it as fuel for your self-improvement journey. You won't achieve your Exceptional Living Plan unless you free yourself from the mental shackles of fear and self-doubt.

A coaching client of mine, Cheri, provides an illustration of the dangers of lack of self-empowerment. Cheri called me not long ago to talk about a promotion that she'd been offered. She said she was inclined to pass because she didn't have enough experience, she'd only been at the company for a short time, and all her predecessors had been male. I asked her about her past successes and the requirements of the new job, and it became clear to me that she was fully capable of performing it well; she just didn't believe in herself enough. Once I explained this to her, she agreed to accept the promotion. When we talked a few weeks later, she told me how much she was enjoying herself. Taking on this new position has been critical in helping Cheri achieve her life goals of greater self-reliance and career success.

When you're empowered, you are more easily able to overcome problems and achieve enhancements to your Exceptional Living Plan. You're paving the way for a smooth entry into the Purpose Zone.

Personal empowerment is predicated on the following beliefs:

- We possess incredible talent, energy, and intelligence just waiting to be unleashed.
- The nature of talent, energy, and intelligence is internal and has a spiritual origin.
- Most of us do not recognize and/or understand how to become empowered.

- We have let others disempower us.
- We are not empowered in the same ways and therefore must find our own mantras.
- We have the ability to empower others.

The following are just a few ideas of specific actions you can take to empower yourself.

Build Self-Confidence

Write down a list of all your best characteristics. What are you most proud of about yourself? You can list big things like major life accomplishments (a college degree, your job, your kids), as well as little things like your eyes or your ability to cook a delicious meal. Carry the list with you on an index card in your wallet at all times. Whenever you are feeling down, or even when you are feeling pretty good about yourself, get out the list and look at it. Take a moment to consider how blessed you are, and how proud you are of putting in the effort to improve your life even more. Do this as often as you can stand. Make appreciating your good qualities a regular habit.

Drive Out Fear

Fear gets in the way of decision making and prevents us from moving forward. We drive it out by drawing upon our abundant inner resources of courage. Some people mistakenly think that courage is reserved for only special people like firefighters and police officers. But we all have the capacity to be courageous. Just think of the numerous everyday heroes who emerged during the events of 9/11. A group of people on the final hijacked plane, upon hearing about what had happened to the Twin Towers, forced their own vessel down in Pennsylvania in order to prevent the terrorists from crashing it into a large building. Their heroic actions saved innocent lives.

The next time you feel afraid of making changes in your life, refer to your Platinum Standard. Refuse to abandon the core principles that you laid down for yourself at the beginning of this program even when you feel that you are failing. Instead, make the time to engage in active meditation.

Sit down in a quiet place. Breathe deeply in and out through your nose several times. When distracting thoughts arise like "What should I make for dinner?" gently push them aside, telling your mind, "Not now." Once you feel that you have cleared your head, envision yourself leading the life that you've always dreamed of. Picture as many of the details as you can: the way your body looks when you weigh 10 pounds less and have toned your muscles from working out at the gym; the feel of your child's arms around you as you grow closer to him; the smile on your mother's face when you make the extra time to spend a Sunday afternoon with her. Do not question yourself or your ability to achieve these goals. Stay focused on picturing them as reality. Feel the positive emotions as they warm your heart, and embrace them. Now imagine a core of light and strength rising up from your chest and spreading out into the world until it forms a protective bubble of energy around you. Revel in the good feelings for as long as you can. When you have completed the meditation, slowly open your eyes and return to your daily life. But hold on to the image of the life you'll have once you've attained your goals. And every time that you feel scared or overwhelmed, envision that bubble of positive energy surrounding you, providing you with the courage to meet life's challenges.

Replace Negative Thought Patterns with Positive Ones

Monitor your self-talk — the constant chatter that runs through your mind every waking moment of your life. Notice every time you speak to yourself in negative, defeatist language. You may even want to create a data sheet to track how often you do this. Now train yourself to use positive language instead. Rather than saying, "I can't do this," say "I can." Rather than saying, "This is unfair," or "I can't believe this is happening to me," say, "I can handle this. I can rise above this." Rehearse and repeat these positive phrases as often as you remember. It may sound silly, but it works. A study conducted with 14-year-olds in inner-city Detroit showed that after just two weeks of doing this assignment, their outlook on life had improved significantly.

In addition, if you feel that you have some major hurdles to overcome in building your self-esteem and achieving your life goals, such as traumas from your past or a particularly challenging relationship in your life today, then I recommend engaging in deeper psychological work. You might consider working with a therapist or life coach to identify and resolve key issues from your past. You might read other self-help books that delve specifically into your core areas of concern. Or you might choose to embark on a dedicated path of meditation or spiritual practice, according to your personal belief system. While such journeys can be immensely challenging, they frequently result in major breakthroughs in your ability to understand what motivates you and see yourself in a more positive light. As a result, these methods often enhance your ability to improve all aspects of your life.

And if you're hitting a wall in terms of your commitment to yourself, remember your customers. You can empower them to help you, and they can free you to be the best person you can be.

ACTIVITY: Outsourcing

When a high-tech company realizes that it's engaged in activities — such as manufacturing or shipping — that are not within the range of its core competency of product development, it outsources them. It takes the work to companies that can do the job better, faster, and cheaper than it can. The businesses that get the work are delighted to have the new business, and the high-tech company itself is able to concentrate its efforts on doing what it does best: communicating with customers about their needs, fostering creativity within its own organization, and therefore developing the most innovative products that it can. The arrangement benefits everyone involved.

Similarly, you can empower others as well as yourself by delegating tasks to them that are taking up too much of your limited resources. Doing this allows you to build their self-esteem and, at the same time, free up time for yourself so that you can truly enter the Purpose Zone. Why not involve other people in helping you implement your Exceptional Living Plan? You don't have to do it alone. Call on the people you're closest to for assistance.

The funny thing is, we're often reluctant to give up control over even minor areas of our life. When we think of empowering others, we often mistakenly believe it means giving our power away. This can prove very threatening: If I give you power, that must mean I have less power. It must then follow that I am less in control and less important. But that is simply not the case. For example, I used to manage the household finances entirely because I like to balance the checkbook to the penny, whereas my wife, Catherine, is of the "close enough" school of thought. And yet when I finally decided to trust her to do the finances herself, she proved an excellent bookkeeper. She was happy to have the added responsibility, and I had more free time to spend just relaxing with her, which was one of my short-term goals. The crucial lesson I learned from this experience was that empowering my wife benefited *both* of us.

When you find yourself overwhelmed, out of time and energy, and generally unable to accomplish your life goals, consider outsourcing. Here's how:

1. Take a look at your Exceptional Living Plan. Remind yourself of your Platinum Standard and your top priorities. Then think about how you're currently living your life. Are you engaged in any activities that are not directly helping you achieve your vision? Are you wasting time on activities that someone else could do better, faster, and cheaper? If so, then you should outsource. These tasks might include household chores such as washing the dishes and mowing the lawn, managing finances, planning vacations, doing home improvements, and caring for your child.

2. Consider whether you might be able to economically hire a professional to do the task for you. For example, I used to struggle for weeks every year to prepare my family's taxes. Finally, one year, Catherine convinced me that we should hire a CPA to do our taxes for us. Although I had to pay him a few hundred dollars, his services were unquestionably worthwhile in terms of my saved time and reduced stress.

3. If hiring someone isn't an option, figure out which of your customers you might be able to ask to take on the tasks. Keep in mind that the goal is not to *force* other people into doing things, but rather to help them develop their potential. Try to choose tasks that you think they'll enjoy and learn from, and then make a positive case for why they should do it.

4. Set expectations. Be clear about what needs to be done and what kind of results you anticipate. Discuss how they'll manage the process on an ongoing basis.
5. Now let them go to it. Try not to interfere. If you do, you're not really empowering them, are you?

The key to successful empowerment is realizing that every one of us has vast reservoirs of talent and energy just waiting to be tapped. It's a crucial step on your path to entering the Purpose Zone.

The A-Plus Player

Entering the Purpose Zone

You have created your Exceptional Living Plan, and you have been working hard to implement it. You've reached many milestones by solving some big problems as well as smaller ones, paying attention to your customers' needs, and enlisting the assistance of others in helping you achieve your goals. You've moved out of the Crisis Zone. By this time, you should be finding a better balance between your work and personal life, and you should be building stronger relationships with your loved ones. These are no small feats.

So the questions I'd like you to ask yourself now are these: "Have I set my sights high enough? Am I really doing the best job at the business of living that I could possibly be doing, and avoiding settling for less? Have I created the conditions necessary to execute the uber-goals that I've envisioned? Am I ready to stop leading an average life and start leading an exceptional one?"

Our natural human tendency is to try to get by with what's *good enough.* After all, "To err is human," right? And so we tend to accept a certain level of waste, mistakes, and errors in our personal lives. I notice, for example, that I avoid taking 30 minutes to read instruction manuals for new technology that I've purchased because I think that I'll be able to figure it out for myself. Reading the manual feels like a waste of time. But then I end up struggling for weeks or even months trying to figure out how to make the latest gadget work. And I always end up thinking to myself, "I should've read the manual!" Taking that 30 minutes out of my busy life up front could have saved me hours of frustration and confusion down the road.

With this milestone, you choose not to accept "good enough" any longer. You say good-bye to "average" and hello to "exceptional." You exit the Complacency Zone, cross the threshold to the Purpose Zone, and become an A-plus player. A-plus players have problems just as you and I, but they keep things in perspective. They target not just filling the minimal requirements in life, but doing their personal best by reaching for their uber-goals. No matter what type of role they play — at home, at work, in their community — they raise the bar for the rest of us.

Rachel, one of my coaching clients, provides an outstanding example of what I'm talking about. A few years ago, Rachel was working full time in Atlanta and, with her husband, raising four kids in the suburbs. But when she was diagnosed with breast cancer, she decided to quit her job. She realized that the stress of balancing her big-time city career and a demanding home life had been too much for her body to handle. The mastectomy left her feeling totally depleted, but she was strong and recovered quickly. When she was ready to get back to work, she started working part time at a place close to home. She wasn't earning as much money as she had in the city, but the family was able to survive off of Rachel and her husband's joint incomes. Rachel was pleased to have more time with her family. Things were looking up.

But then tragedy struck again. Rachel's husband, Tom, was diagnosed with a rare blood disease that can be fatal at any time. He was forced to stop working, and Rachel was forced to become the family's sole wage earner. Fortunately, Tom was healthy enough to be a stay-at-home dad, and so he took over running the household.

When Rachel came to me for advice on how to handle this challenge, she wasn't bitter or depressed. She was in no way ready to give up. I admired her ability to make the best of her situation. But she did feel torn. On the one hand, she knew that the best way to support her family would be to go back to a full-time job in Atlanta. Plus she admitted to me that she was actually excited to get back on the fast track, which, to be honest, she'd kind of missed. On the other hand, she knew that her cancer was still only in remission, not fully cured, and she didn't want to jeopardize her health by taking on a job that was too stressful. She had also been greatly enjoying the extra time she'd been getting to spend with her family since starting to work part time.

After listening to Rachel talk about her priorities and needs, I suggested that she go for the big city job but negotiate with her employer to spend three days a week working in the city and the other two days working from home. That way, she'd be able to earn a high salary and get the excitement of her old job back, but save commute time two days a week. She could use this time to relax with her family and take care of herself.

Rachel took my recommendation, and, thankfully, the company agreed to her requests. She got it all: the big job, the big bucks, *and* two days a week working at home. Rachel certainly isn't out of the woods — Tom's blood disease could get worse at any time. But she is my own personal hero for what she has been able to achieve and how she has been able to stick to her Platinum Standard in spite of the obstacles life has put in her path. She is truly an A-plus player. She is living in the Purpose Zone: realizing her personal dreams while always making her loved ones her highest priority. Talk about exceptional living!

We shouldn't strive for perfection in our lives; we'll just drive ourselves crazy. But we should challenge ourselves, like Rachel, to be the best that we can be. In so doing, we'll take ourselves to the ultimate level of quality living.

Here's an activity designed to help you become an A-plus player.

ACTIVITY: Supercharge Me!

In consulting with businesses and individuals who are attempting to go beyond the ordinary and become A-plus players, I recommend **Supercharging.** When you Supercharge, you write a credo declaring what you're setting out to accomplish — your uber-goal — and what that enhancement will do to improve your life.

However, before you start Supercharging, please make sure you're up for the task. You should be solidly out of short-term crisis mode and moving into the Purpose Zone before taking on any of your uber-goals. Supercharging is done with your long-term vision in mind. It requires thinking beyond right now and into the future. It means moving closer and closer to living your life in accordance with your Platinum Standard, to living an exceptional life as an A-plus player. If you're still struggling to make your daily life less chaotic, or dealing with a major transition, perhaps you should hold off on this step for the moment.

Now, if you're ready, here's how to Supercharge. Consider the uber-goals that you listed on your Exceptional Living Plan. Challenge yourself to achieve at least one of these uber-goals in the near future. If not, your uber-goals may never become reality. They may remain in the abstract realm of "I wish" rather than in the concrete realm of "I can." Do this not because it is necessary, but because it will add an extra degree of satisfaction and personal fulfillment to your life.

Next, write your Supercharge Me! Credo. The credo should describe three things:

1. Your current habit or state of being.
2. Your uber-goal, stated in present tense.
3. The positive impact reaching this goal will have on your life.

Here are a couple of examples of credos that clients or students of mine have written:

- "I'm currently averaging seven petty arguments per week with my family members. Over the next 60 days, I am reducing the number of petty arguments to zero. This will eliminate tension and enhance goodwill."
- "I now work as a mid-level manager at a large organization. In the next few years, I will be promoted to vice president of my division. In this role, I will earn more money and feel better about my accomplishments."
- "I am frustrated by my reluctance to take risks. I will go skydiving within the next month. This will allow me to overcome my fears, so that I will be willing to take bigger risks in other aspects of my life."

As you can see from these examples, your Supercharge Me! credos can concern big or small changes—they're all stair steps on your way to achieving your life vision. Just be sure to define your projects in a measurable way so that you can track your progress. And then remember to actually collect the necessary data and record your accomplishments on your Exceptional Living Plan.

Don't feel as though you need to accomplish every goal —
and certainly not every uber-goal — on your Exceptional
Living Plan right away. Instead, I'd suggest committing
to two or three major projects at a time, some larger and
some smaller in scope. The most important part of becoming an A-plus player is having the right attitude. If
you've committed to serving others and achieving your
best, then, in a very critical way, you've already begun leading an exceptional life.

Interlude

By accomplishing the first 10 milestones, you've solved problems to exit the Crisis Zone, focused attention on your key customers to leave the Complacency Zone, and empowered yourself to achieve your highest goals in order to enter the Purpose Zone. Go back to the Introduction, and complete the Quality-of-Life Index again. Is your score higher? It should have improved substantially since the first time you took the assessment, and measurably since the last time you took it. Record your score so that you can compare your results again later.

Phase IV

Keeping Your Momentum Going

Your Exceptional Living Plan is a work in progress—that's why I call it a living plan. *If you don't continue to update and implement your plan by setting new goals as you achieve the old ones and making adjustments as your circumstances change, then you risk quickly backsliding into an average life. You've exorcised your demons (your bad habits), but unless you nurture your new positive spirit, the demons will come back—and they'll be meaner than ever. You have raised your standards. Keeping those standards high requires constant vigilance.*

In this one-week phase, you'll learn to keep your momentum going by embracing the spirit of continuous improvement.

The Only Constant in Life Is Change

Embracing the Spirit of Continuous Improvement

Mike is a new dad who works full time in Ohio. When asked to describe his life when we first met, he said, "Frenetic, stressful, hectic." When asked to talk about the life he wanted, he said, "In the short term, I want to make time for my kids. And in the long term, I want to buy a house for my family." So I helped him make and execute a plan to do just that. Mike set goals for putting away a percentage of his paycheck every month by packing home lunches, making fewer frivolous purchases, and consolidating his debt. In just over a year, he had already saved enough money to make a down payment.

But an exceptional life is a never-ending journey and requires continuous improvement. Even though he's been able to achieve one of his long-term goals, Mike is not done. Rather, he is ready to move on to the next goal. He and I are currently working on tackling his next big goal: spending more time with his new baby.

Life isn't perfect—and neither are we. Sometimes we try our best but things still don't turn out the way we'd hoped. Even when we do meet with success, life is always in flux. Remember Rachel? She successfully battled breast cancer only to discover that her husband had a rare blood disease and she had to go back to work full time. In the course of implementing your Exceptional Living Plan, you'll overcome obstacles, but you'll also face unanticipated challenges. Your desires and needs will change, as will those of your Gold, Silver, and Bronze Circle customers.

Therefore, there is no end point at which you will complete your Exceptional Living Plan. It is a living document, and will constantly evolve over time. *But it also will enable you to handle anything that comes your way.*

I encourage you to view this book not as a one-time read, something that you've finished and can now put aside. Rather, think of the methodology that you've implemented and the activities you've conducted while reading *Me, Inc.* as an entirely new skill set for managing your life. Keep returning to your Exceptional Living Plan on a regular basis, and you'll find that you're able to take on all of life's challenges—from starting a new job or relationship, to breaking up, to growing older, to dealing with illness—with more grace and ease. It's like meditation: You practice the breathing techniques not just so that you can sit quietly for a few minutes every morning, but so that you can calm yourself down when you're stuck in traffic or arguing with your partner. You can apply your skills from here forward, whenever you're facing a transition, making a difficult decision, or just trying to reach a new level of personal achievement.

Jennifer took my course at Fordham University over six years ago, but she still makes use of her Exceptional Living Plan to this day. There's no question that, as the CFO of a major media company, Jennifer has achieved a high degree of success in her professional life. But thanks to the lessons she learned in class, she's also made balancing work with her personal life a top priority.

Jennifer reviews and updates her Exceptional Living Plan at least once a year. "It's a great motivator — it keeps me pursuing my goals and setting new ones," she says. "Plus, every time I read my Platinum Standard, I'm reminded of the fact that I want to be spending more time with my friends and family and can't let my career take over."

The last time she revisited her plan, Jennifer discovered that she had accomplished all of her major goals, including reaching the level of senior executive at work, losing weight, learning Italian, and becoming closer to her ailing father. "It made me feel great," she told me. "That's what I wanted to do, and I did it! I really am leading an exceptional life."

Take a look at your Exceptional Living Plan. Have you accomplished the major milestones? Knocked out some of your goals? Solved a couple of problems? Even perhaps achieved an uber-goal? How are you living your life in comparison to your Platinum Standard? If you've achieved even a few of your Must-Haves, then you are well on your way to living a more purposeful, fulfilling life. Take a moment to feel good about what you've accomplished.

Now consider whether any of your priorities have changed. Perhaps you've decided to start a family, for example. This may require you to move the career achievement and intellectual stimulation categories further down your Priority Pyramid and the relationships category further up. Don't be afraid to change your strategic imperatives and revise your goals as a consequence of this shift: Spending more time at home will probably be more important to you now than getting a promotion. The only thing that shouldn't change is your Platinum Standard.

The more frequently you update your Exceptional Living Plan, the better. It means that you're keeping on top of life's changes. You're embracing the spirit of continuous improvement.

However, it can be difficult to stay motivated if you're going at it alone. It makes sense to enlist the assistance of others to help you keep focused on your self-improvement efforts. Here's an activity that will allow you to do just that.

ACTIVITY: This Is Your Life

At work, performance appraisals are critical. Without them, you wouldn't know what you were doing well, what your areas for improvement were, or what to expect in the future. Of course, sometimes they can be unpleasant if the feedback is delivered in a negative way. But overall, most of us understand and appreciate the importance of reviewing our work on a regular basis.

It used to be that performance appraisals were a simple matter of an employee sitting down for some one-on-one feedback with his or her boss. But recently, companies have started using a methodology known as 360-degree feedback. This means that you get reviewed not just by your boss, but by employees working for you, colleagues at your level, and other supervisors as well. This system provides a far more accurate and balanced picture of your total performance on the job.

I'd recommend taking the 360-degree feedback approach in evaluating how well you're accomplishing your Exceptional Living Plan. Ask your most important customers for their input. You might even consider giving them a copy of your Exceptional Living Plan. This may sound pretty intimidating, I'll admit. But if you really want to know how you're doing, it's the best way to find out.

I had one student, Alex, who sent out an e-mail to everyone in his life who knew him well — his parents, grandparents, siblings, friends, and closest colleagues — asking them for specific feedback. He loved getting their valuable input. What's more, he felt like after having filled out the evaluation, these customers were better equipped to help him implement his Exceptional Living Plan because they understood better what he was trying to accomplish.

Requesting feedback doesn't have to be a complicated process. Just list all your priorities and the Must-Haves for each one. For example, your "performance evaluation" form might look something like this:

How well would you say I'm achieving my goals in each of the following areas?
   Please rate on a scale from 1 to 5 (1 = not well, 3 = neutral, 5 = very well):

Relationships:
- Spend more time with family. _____
- Talk to friends more often. _____

Emotional well-being:
- Take more mini-vacations. _____
- Stop being so hard on myself. _____

Intellectual stimulation:
- Read fewer trashy magazines. _____
- Learn Italian. _____

You should do "This Is Your Life" every six months. I e-mail my students six months after they complete my course to remind them that it's time for their first one. Since you won't be getting an e-mail from me, I urge you to set up some sort of reminder system now. Put it in your Palm Pilot to repeat on a quarterly basis and set an alarm. Mark it on your calendar. Just do it.

Regularly reviewing your progress toward attaining the goals you set forth in your Exceptional Living Plan will help you stay focused and motivated. Keep up the good work.

♛

To be sure, striving for continuous improvement does not guarantee an easy or blissful life. In fact, it requires sacrifices, trade-offs, hard decisions, and even suffering. But fortunately happiness is not the aim, nor is perfection. Living a life of purpose is about achieving a sense of spiritual fulfillment. It's about feeling as though you're operating in accordance with your values. It's about knowing, at the end of your life, that you've done your best.

When asked to think of individuals who strove throughout their lives for continuous improvement, many of us name famous people such as Gandhi, Martin Luther King Jr., and Mother Teresa. I agree that these icons serve as standards of excellence. But the world is filled with ordinary people like you and me who make a conscious decision to improve our lives and the lives of others every day. And we are just as important in making the world a better place, not just for ourselves but for our children and our children's children.

George Bernard Shaw summed it up aptly in *Man and Superman*:

> This is the true joy of life, the being used for a purpose recognized by yourself as a mighty one; the being a force of nature instead of a feverish, selfish, little clod of ailments and grievances complaining

that the world will not devote itself to making you happy. . . . I am of the opinion that my life belongs to the whole community and as long as I live it is my privilege to do for it whatever I can. . . . I want to be thoroughly used up when I die, for the harder I work the more I live. I rejoice in life for its own sake. Life is no "brief candle" to me. It is a sort of splendid torch which I have got hold of for the moment, and I want to make it burn as brightly as possible before handing it on to future generations.

Epilogue

Would You Follow You?

Being a Leader

Just by picking up this book, you've taken a courageous step in your life: You've expressed a desire for self-improvement. By now, you've created an Exceptional Living Plan to help you achieve your goals and you've begun the process of implementing it. Finally, you've set yourself on the path of a lifetime of continuous improvement, always striving for the exceptional rather than the average. What more could there possibly be to living a purposeful, quality life?

You can take yourself even a step beyond the scope of this book by deciding to be a leader. This means taking responsibility for your own life, having confidence in your abilities, and maintaining your motivation even when times get tough. It also means pushing your own selfish needs aside and focusing more on the needs of your key customers. Being a leader requires us to shed our preconceived ideas of power, authority, and control, replacing them with humility, forgiveness, and love.

Conventional wisdom states that people are born leaders . . . or not. I disagree. Leadership is not just for a designated few. There are many examples of people who were forced to take on leadership roles out of necessity — not out of desire — and flourished in doing so. Mary Kay Ash, for example, *had* to start earning money when her husband walked out on her and her three kids. Talk about a Burning Platform! Eventually, she founded Mary Kay Cosmetics, now a two-billion-dollar company.

Identify someone in a leadership position whom you admire. What are his or her primary characteristics? Write down which traits you would like to work harder to emulate in your own life. Then make a plan for cultivating those qualities in yourself.

Remember, you are the CEO of Me, Inc. If you were an employee of the company, would you follow you?

♛

Taking control of our own lives has never been as challenging, or as important, as it is today. Our personal and professional roles require substantially greater self-management skills than were ever demanded of our predecessors. We can no longer depend on our employers or our partners to provide for us. We must be self-reliant. But isn't it ironic that businesses have unwittingly given us the principles and tools to help us compete in this insecure, unpredictable new world? Thanks to their efforts to make their companies more successful, we have a model for personal transformation!

Acknowledgments

This book has evolved over a 20-year period. Over those years, numerous people have provided support and guidance. I am especially grateful to those who have provided special encouragement. Thanks first go to my friend and mentor, Professor Jim Stoner of Fordham University's Graduate School of Business. It was Jim who invited me to teach at Fordham on the "Me, Inc." principles back in 1993. Since then, he also gently pushed me to complete this manuscript. Thanks to the hundreds of Fordham graduate students who attended my course, offering their insights and wisdom, including Dawn Brock, Paul Robinson, Derek Whitehead, and Terri Lombardi, who inspired the book title. A very special thank-you goes to MeiMei Fox, who is a naturally gifted writer — she worked shoulder to shoulder with me to develop and perfect the original manuscript into its current form. Thanks to Heidi Yeranossian, Lisa Hyman, and Emily Navarro for their editorial assistance, and to Teri Schindler, another very gifted writer and friend, who helped create widespread interest in "Me, Inc." Thanks to all my corporate